Problem Regions of Europe
General Editor **D. I. Scargill**

The Scandinavian Northlands
W. R. Mead

Oxford University Press

Oxford University Press, Ely House, London W.1

Glasgow New York Toronto Melbourne Wellington
Cape Town Ibadan Nairobi Dar es Salaam Lusaka Addis Ababa
Delhi Bombay Calcutta Madras Karachi Lahore Dacca
Kuala Lumpur Singapore Hong Kong Tokyo

© Oxford University Press 1974

First published 1974
Reprinted 1975

I am grateful to Ilmari Hustich, Harald Meltzer, and William William-Olsson for helpful comments on the text, and to Kenneth Wass for assistance with the maps and diagrams.
W.R.M.

Filmset by BAS Printers Limited, Wallop, Hampshire
and printed in Great Britain
at the University Press, Oxford
by Vivian Ridler, Printer to the University

Editor's Preface

Great economic and social changes have taken place in Europe in recent years. The agricultural workforce in the west was halved, for example, during the 1950s and 1960s. This unprecedented flight from the land has made possible some much-needed reorganization of farm holdings but it has also created problems, not least that of finding uses for land in the highlands and elsewhere where it is no longer profitable to farm. Closely related is the difficulty of maintaining services to a much diminished rural population or of providing new kinds of services for the week-enders or holidaymakers who have tended increasingly to buy up rural properties as they have come on the market. In some places the demands of this new population have been difficult to reconcile with those of the more traditional rural dwellers.

Contraction of the labour force has also taken place in many old-established industries including coal- and iron-mining and such manufacturing industries as shipbuilding, railway engineering, wool and cotton textiles, and leather. The coalmining industry alone has shed something like two-thirds of its workforce since 1950, the effect of competition from other fuels having been made more severe by the adoption of automation, which has replaced men by machines in the collieries that survive. The problems have been especially serious in those coalfields or manufacturing districts that have a high level of dependence on a single source of employment—a not uncommon consequence of Europe's industrial past—and the efforts of those who seek to attract new industries to replace the old are often thwarted by a legacy of pollution, ugliness, bad housing, and soured labour relations.

Quite a different set of problems has arisen in the great cities of Europe such as London and Paris, and in the conurbations of closely linked cities well exemplified by Randstad Holland, the Ring City. Here the problems arise from growth: growth that has been brought about by the expansion of consumer-orientated manufacturing and even more by the massive increase of white-collar office jobs that proliferate in 'down-town' business districts. The problems are economic, social, and political, and they include the effects of congestion, of soaring land and property values, of the growing divorce of place of residence from place of work, and the difficulty of administering and planning a metropolitan region that may be shared between many independently-minded local authorities. Yet the city continues to attract migrants and decentralization schemes founder on the residents' reluctance to leave the 'bright lights', the familiar shops or football club.

The problems resulting from change are not passing ones. Despite the best endeavours of politicians and planners they exhibit a persistence which amply justifies their study on an areal basis. Hence the *Problem Regions of Europe* series. The volumes in this series have all been written by geographers who, by the nature of their discipline, may be expected to take a broadly-based approach to description and analysis. Geographers in the past have been reluctant to base their studies on problem regions since the problem was often of a temporary nature, less enduring than the 'personality' of the region. Yet such is the magnitude of the problems referred to above that the geographer would seem to be well justified in approaching his regional study by seeking to identify, measure, and even seek solutions to problems. Indeed it has been suggested that regions themselves can be defined in terms of the problems with which they are confronted.

Certain themes emerge clearly when the basis of the problem is examined: the effects of a harsh environment, of remoteness, and of political division, as well as of industrial decay or urban congestion. One or other of these major problems forms the dominant theme in each of the volumes in the series. But these have not been considered in isolation and the studies that make up the series have been carefully chosen in order that comparisons can be made both in terms of the causes that give rise to persistent problems and of the solutions that are sought for them. Thus, for example, both the Italian Mezzogiorno and Andalusia in Spain have to contend with the problems of Mediterranean drought, wind, and flood, but the precise nature of these and other problems, as well as man's response to them, differs in the two regions. Similarly, the response to economic change is not the same in North-East England as in North Rhine–Westphalia, nor the response to social pressures the same in Paris as in the Randstad.

Although the treatment of each subject varies according to the nature of the region concerned and, to some extent, the outlook of a particular author, readers will find much in common in the arrangement of contents in each volume. In each of them the nature of the problem or problems which characterize the region is first stated by the author; next the circumstances that have given rise to the problems are explained; after this the methods that have been employed to overcome the problems are subjected to critical examination and evaluation. Particular attention is paid to the efforts which individual governments have made to grapple with their planning problems.

Governments have long been aware of the problems resulting from economic and social changes and various attempts have been made to solve them. Development Areas and New Towns in Great Britain, for example, represent an attempt to deal with the problems, on the one hand, of declining industrial areas and, on the other, of the overgrown cities. Such solutions can hardly be described as regional, however. Other countries have recognized the problems of their overpopulated rural areas and the Cassa per il Mezzogiorno, the Fund for the South, was set up by the Italian government in 1950 in order to encourage investment in the South. The E.E.C. has also channelled funds via its Investment Bank, both to southern Italy and to other parts of the Common Market distant from the main centres of economic activity. Planning of this kind shows an awareness of the regional extent of economic and social problems, although in practice the policies followed have too often been piecemeal and short-term. Motives were good, but success was limited by the lack of an overall regional strategy that would have treated small areas and their particular local problems in the context of a much bigger unit which had positive advantages to offer as well as problems.

Since about 1960, however, the continuing nature of the problems has persuaded most European governments to adopt longer-term and more comprehensive planning measures, and the importance of seeking regional solutions has been stressed. The last ten years have, in fact, witnessed the setting up of regional planning authorities in many European countries and to them has been given the task of identifying regional problems and of finding solutions to them. Economic Planning Regions were defined in Britain in 1964 and although their Boards have no legislative powers, they have nevertheless produced some useful advisory documents. Other European countries have adopted similar regional frameworks, the French planning regions, for example, dating from 1963. The idea of the *métropoles d' équilibre* is also to introduce new vigour to the regions via the largest provincial towns. Such evidence as this suggests that planning strategy in the future will be implemented increasingly within a regional framework. The E.E.C. is also seeking to work out a regional policy, whilst continuing to help with its funds and expertise those problem areas that are already the concern of national governments.

The move towards regional planning at both national and international levels makes particularly timely the appearance of the *Problem Regions of Europe* series and authors have sought to explore the success or otherwise of the policies that have already been formulated. Two other trends provide additional reasons for launching the series. One of these is the movement to reform the out-dated boundaries of local government areas, substituting bigger units for the small and frequently anomalous divisions that were created in the nineteenth century. Another is a revival of popular interest in regions, their history, industrial archaeology, customs, and dialect. This latter development is seen by some as a reaction against excessive State centralization and the uniformity of life that stems from mass media, advertising, and the emergence of a common culture.

All the authors of the series have considerable first-hand knowledge of the regions about which they have written. Yet none of them would claim to have a complete set of answers to any particular regional problem. For this reason, as well as from a desire to make the series challenging, each volume contains suggestions for further lines of inquiry that the reader may pursue. When it was first planned the *Problem Region* series was rather modestly thought of as useful to the sixth-form student of geography. As it has progressed it has become clear that the authors have contributed studies that will be valuable not only for sixth-form work, but also as a basis for the more detailed investigations undertaken by advanced students, both of geography and of European studies in general.

D.I.S.

St. Edmund Hall, Oxford
August 1973

Contents

1 The Setting
Nordkalotten—A new concept in Norden   7
The point of view   7
The character of Nordkalotten   8
The impact of new technologies   10
The principle of comparative disadvantage   11

2 Social Problems
'The Kingdom of Lapland'   12
The distribution of population   14

3 Economic Problems
The nature of the raw materials   21
  Fisheries   21
  Forests   22
  Minerals   22
  Hydro-electric power   23
  Farming   24
The organizational framework   25

4 Political Problems
Internal considerations   27
  Mental attitudes   27
  Ethnographic issues   28
External considerations   30
  Boundaries in Nordkalotten   30
  The strategic situation of Nordkalotten   30

5 The Search for Solutions
Political solutions   33
Economic solutions   33
Administrative solutions   40
The illusion of logical structures   44

6 The Way of the Four Winds   45

Further Work   47

Index   48

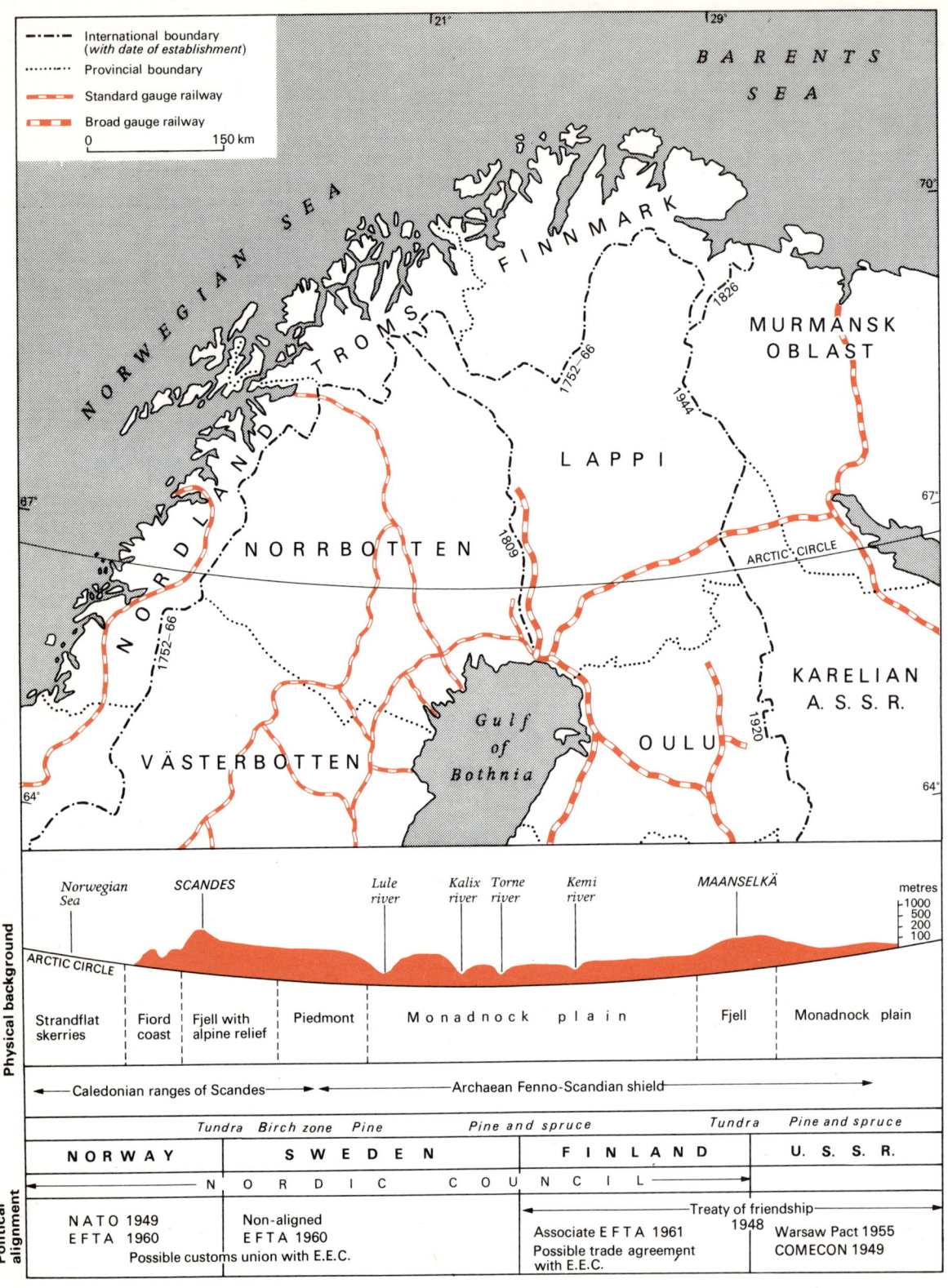

Fig. 1. A transect through Nordkalotten

1 The Setting

Nordkalotten—A new concept in Norden

Since the Second World War, the northernmost part of Norway, Sweden, and Finland has acquired sufficient prominence to make it worthy of attention in its own right. It is anything but a uniform area and it has anything but unity. Indeed, it is a territory of pronounced contrasts in which the differences between the areas belonging to Norway, Sweden, and Finland substantially outweigh the likenesses. Furthermore, the differences inherent in the physical geography of the area have been exaggerated by political divisions. Yet there are common factors to which attention is directed for political and economic as well as military reasons. In identifying the problems that result from the changing status of and situation in northern Scandinavia, the area has been accorded a measure of personification. It has been christened Nordkalotten (Pohjoiskalotti, in Finnish; Nuor'ta Kalot'ta, in Lappish).

The name is of recent provenance. It has been in use since the Second World War, but encyclopaedias suggest that it has only been given wider currency since the late 1950s when it was used by the Nordic Council. Two translations for Nordkalotten have been employed: 'the northern cap' and 'the European north calotte': neither is very successful. The name owes its origin to the cartographic shape of the area. It resembles the round cap or calotte worn by a priest. The resemblance is the more striking if Nordkalotten is viewed in its narrower context as those parts of Norway, Sweden, and Finland that fall within the Arctic Circle.

Nordkalotten has different meanings for different groups of people. The Arctic Circle inscribes an arc which cuts through the Finnish county of Lappi, the Swedish county of Norrbotten, and the Norwegian county of Nordland. Most of those who use the term would consider it to embrace extensive territories lying to the south of the Arctic Circle—certainly the whole of the three units mentioned. Some would include the marginal territories of Västerbotten and Oulu (Uleåborg) counties. Military strategists extend the concept to include adjacent parts of the U.S.S.R. Bonniers' *Lexikon* (1966) also includes the Kola peninsula.

Clearly, Nordkalotten lacks formal definition—so does Lapland. But the territory is already more than a part of the convenient terminology of military strategists. It arouses a variety of images in the mind. With these images there are associated problems. Leaving aside that part of the planned economy of the U.S.S.R. which falls into Nordkalotten, the market economies of Norway, Sweden, and Finland have much to gain by looking at their northern territories unitedly rather than separately. Many of the problems of Nordkalotten are common to the separate polities. It has become increasingly apparent that a combined approach has much to commend it and that remedial measures are more economically applied by collective action.

The point of view

Nordkalotten bristles with problems. It is helpful to view them as the product of interaction between four variables—physical environment, population, technology, and organization. Each variable generates its own group of problems.

The relationship between people and place is expressed largely, but not exclusively, in terms of technology. The relationships between people have their outward forms in systems of organization or administration. Technical processes of invention, with all their many implications for man–land relations, tend to change more quickly than forms of social and economic organization.

This study looks first at the physical characteristics of Nordkalotten and certain technological inventions which have been critical for its transformation. There follows a review of the social, economic, and political problems that confront Nordkalotten. Each set of problems calls for its own solutions; although in the same way as the problems are inseparable from each other, so the solutions to any given set will (1) impinge upon other sets of problems and (2) influence the solutions that are simultaneously being applied to them. In the broader world scene, the Scandinavians have acquired a reputation for being more technically inventive and socially innovative than most peoples. All their technical and social ingenuity is needed to sustain and accommodate within their body politic this sub-Arctic outpost area of Europe.

The character of Nordkalotten

In European terms, Nordkalotten has two basic characteristics. Firstly, however narrowly its geographical limits may be defined, it is an extensive area (Fig. 2). Norway's most northerly counties (*fylker*) of Finnmark, Troms, and Nordland (112 000 sq. km) are as large as Ireland and Wales put together. Sweden's county (*län*) of Norrbotten (99 000 sq. km) and Finland's county (*lääni*) of Lappi (94 000 sq. km) are both larger than Scotland. Secondly, Nordkalotten is one of the remotest parts of the continent. As an aircraft flies most of it is a thousand kilometres from the nearest great concentrations of population. Before air transport was introduced, Luleå was the most accessible town by overland routes, while until the 1930s, express ships on the coastal routes took several days to link the northern ports of Norway with its southern cities.

The difficulties resulting from extensiveness and remoteness are compounded of latitudinal setting and the nature of the terrain. Although the North Atlantic Drift brings modifying warmth to the coastal waters of north Norway so that, for its latitude, the Norwegian littoral experiences some of the most positive temperature anomalies in the world, the effects are rapidly dissipated inland. The quality of light is different from that in lower latitudes. Moonlight, starlight, and light reflected from snow have greater significance (the Lappish 'star pictures' recall a primeval reaction). The Aurora Borealis reaches its maximum in frequency of occurrence in north Norway. The more familiar consequence of high latitude is the seasonal rhythm of daylight and darkness. At Utsjoki, Kirkenes, and Hammerfest, the summer sun does not drop below the horizon for seventy days: the winter night is correspondingly long and there is no compensating spring or lingering autumn.

The exaggerated rhythm of daylight and darkness, with its climatic extremes, is played out on landscapes which are frequently desolate and forbidding, but some of which in summer can break into a deceptively southern smile. Most of Nordkalotten is the product of the Caledonian orogeny, but beyond the piedmont zones of Sweden and Finland it falls to the archaean peneplain of the east that is commonly known as the Fennoscandian Shield. All the Nordkalotten area has experienced heavy and prolonged glaciation, but although much of it is tundra or cold desert country, most of it is of relatively low altitude so that it lacks extensive glaciers or permafrost.

A transect along the line of the Arctic Circle

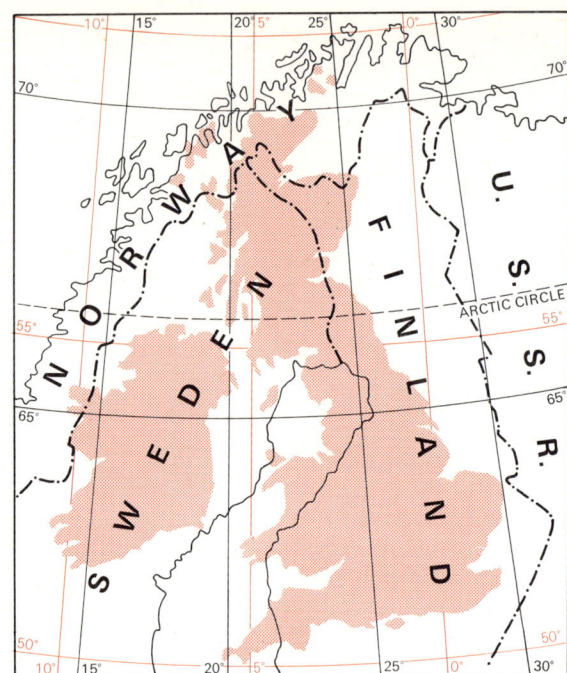

Fig. 2. The British Isles superimposed on Norway, Sweden, and Finland. The maps show comparability of area between the territories

(Fig. 1) will give some indication of the character of the countryside. The western approaches are announced by the fractured skerry guard or *strandflat* of the Nordland coast, the elaborate archipelagoes of which anticipate the lofty fiorded coastline. The boundary between Norway and Sweden is traced mostly across broad plateaux or *vidder* at altitudes which exceed 1500 metres. The *vidder* are high, wide and (depending on the season and the weather) handsome lands. Their scrub vegetation, splendidly colourful in the brief flush of autumn, merges with the Alpine flora and lichens of the higher rock-shatter zone and falls through the gnarled birch and willow groves that mark the descent from the sub-Arctic piedmont to Nordkalotten's coniferous woodlands; for much of Nordkalotten is covered with what the Swedes call *barrskogen*, the needle woods, the pines of which extend higher both latitudinally and altitudinally than the spruce. Through the woodland zone also course the rivers. They are fed by the elongated lake reservoirs of the piedmont, are interrupted by frequent cataracts and rapids, and are flanked by broad suites of terraces. The Big and Little Lule rivers, the Kalix, Muonio, Torne, Ounas, and Kemi all intersect the Arctic Circle, which is formally

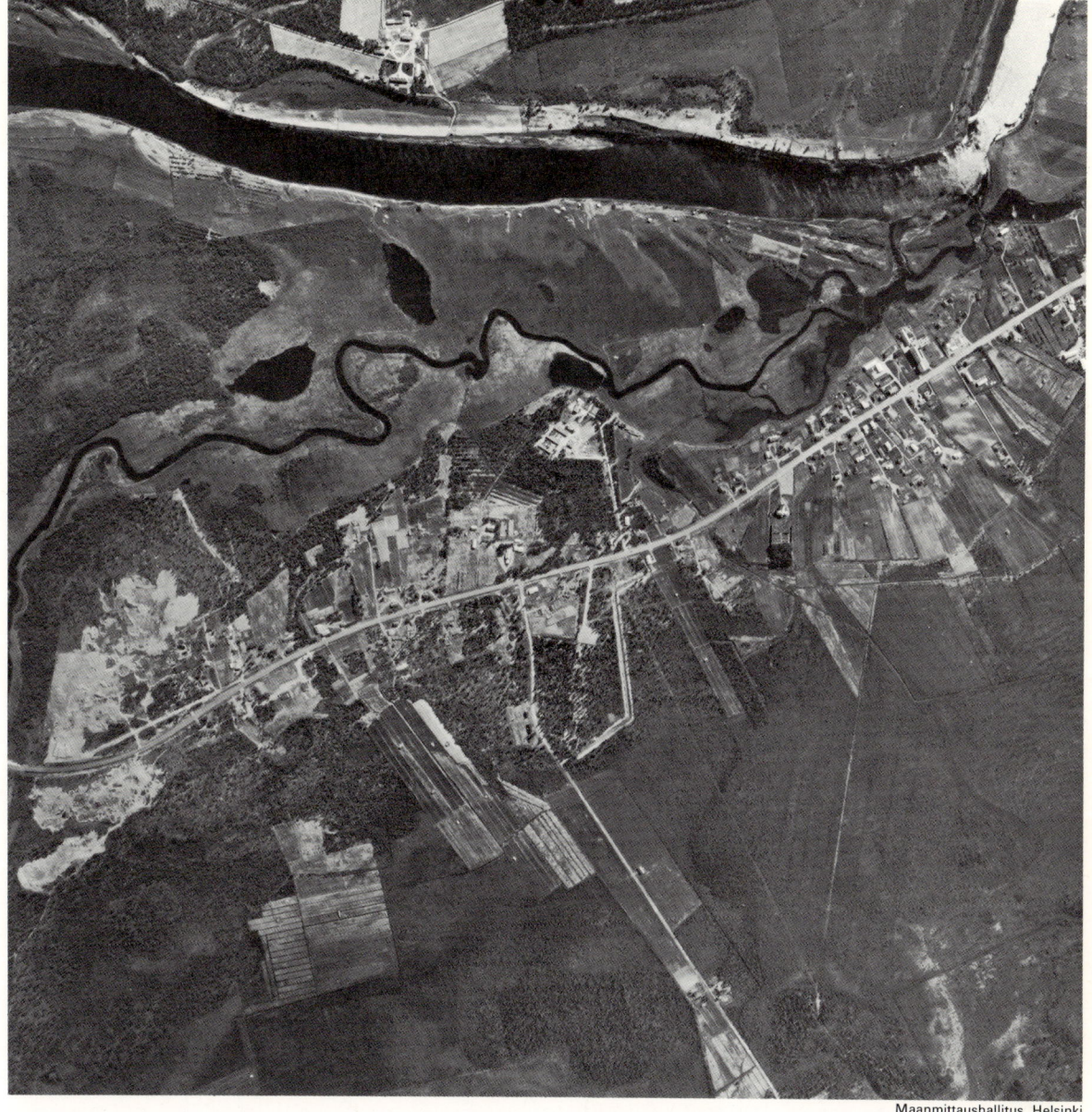

An air photograph of a part of Kittilä parish, Ounas valley, Finnish Lapland. Kittilä lies on the limits of field husbandry and near to the frontiers of satisfactory timber growth. It is from such isolated settlement areas that emigration proceeds vigorously

marked along most of the official routeways. The spurs of the hump-backed fells (or *tunturit*, as they are called on the Finnish side of the border) extend south from the height of land to the interfluves. On the eastern marchlands, where the Arctic Circle passes through the Finnish parish of Salla, rivers that have their headwaters in interior Finland and their outlets on the White Sea coast of Russian Karelia cut gorges through the fells.

Hydrographically, the allegiance of Nordkalotten is divided between outer ocean and inner sea: the tidal, saltwater, ice-free Norwegian Sea which is part of the North Atlantic and gives access to the Barents Sea and the Arctic Ocean; and the non-tidal, brackish, seasonally frozen, virtually enclosed Baltic Sea. Nordkalotten faces the outer ocean, or Western Sea (*Västersjön*) as it was known historically, in a rugged, fiorded coast with great promontories and island groups which

Swedish Iron Ore Co. London

The north of Scandinavia has been in some respects what the west has been to the U.S.A. These are some of the pioneers who helped to lay the railways and to open the mining settlements at the turn of the century

look like drowned Alps in profile. It virtually dissolves into the Bothnian Gulf of the East Sea (*Östersjön*), as the Scandinavians still call it, through low-lying islands, dune fields, skerries, and reefs, which are isostatically active and over which winter ice rides.

In Nordkalotten, the world of nature prevails: the works of man are subordinate. Geographers of two generations ago designated it a region of hardship, a territory where men submitted to the absolutism of natural forces. Its most successful enterprises were those in which men adapted themselves most freely and most fully to natural circumstances. Other than the fishers and hunters who had settled the coastal areas of north Norway since the retreat of ice (and whose litter of artifacts as well as of rock drawings recall the antiquity of settlement) northern Scandinavia was first occupied by the Lapps. They gave to the territory most of the place names that have slowly crystallized on its maps. The culture and the economy of the Lapps may be efficient forms of environmental adjustment, but they represent a lowly standard of life in European terms. North Norway, Sweden, and Finland have always been under-developed, but less under-developed than the image of Lapland suggests. The relative degree of their under-development has been made manifest with the rise of modern technology. It has thrown into relief the inherent differences between north and south: it has created the rudimentary illusion of two nations. The irony is that the very techniques and aids that in theory should reduce the differences, tend to increase them.

The impact of new technologies

The first technical changes to have a direct effect on Nordkalotten were in the field of transport. The steel-plated steamship increased the speed, frequency, and regularity of connections along the Norwegian coast and offered the prospects of a more extended shipping season for ports in the Gulf of Bothnia. The first railway to be constructed in Nordkalotten—the North of Europe Railway Company Ltd.—was financed on a concession granted between Gällivare and Luleå. It opened in 1887. Swedish State Railways extended their standard gauge main line north to Boden in 1894. In 1903 Finnish State Railways opened their broad gauge system to Tornio railhead. Meanwhile, the Swedish Government took over the British concessions and extended the Gällivare line through Kiruna to the Norwegian boundary, where the Norwegians completed the track down to Ofoten fiord in 1903. It was electrified 1920–3. The ore line (*Malmbanan*), a 'proud epic in the wilderness' to the poet Einar Malm, carries the heaviest traffic of any line in Scandinavia. Side by side with the coming of the railway, telephone systems started to penetrate the northern wilderness.

Simultaneously, too, new methods of treating iron ore for steel production had powerful indirect consequences for the high north of Scandinavia. The Gilchrist–Thomas process for the reduction of phosphoric ores was the most important of them, giving an entirely new value to north Sweden's extensive iron ore deposits. The existence of these high-yielding ores had been well known for three centuries, but not until after 1878 could they be effectively processed. A second resource of Nordkalotten experienced revaluation with the evolution of methods for converting softwood timber into pulp and paper. This added a new dimension to the industrialist's view of northern Sweden and Finland, for the new, higher valued, more easily handled goods made it profitable to extend factory enterprises to the head of the Bothnian Gulf. But it was not until the 1940s that all of Sweden's softwood timbers in Nordkalotten were economically accessible and not until the 1960s that the same applied to those of Finland. The third invention critical for Nordkalotten was the invention of the dynamo together with methods of transmitting hydro-electric energy. Realization of its resources, however, had to await the perfection of large-scale methods for harnessing power and of means for its long-distance transmission.

Since the Second World War, the development of cheaper and speedier methods of road construction and maintenance have released social and economic development in northern Scandinavia from locations beside the railway lines and the steamship terminals. Roads to resources have become a reality—and no less importantly the same roads have provided access to services. Nor is the incidence of winter felt so heavily by the transport system with the wider availability of more efficient snow-clearing equipment and ice-combating devices. More personalized forms of mechanical transport have a disproportionate importance for the inhabitants of Nordkalotten: for the fishermen, the relatively cheap motor-boat engine; for the countryman, the tractor to improve his mobility as well as to supplement his labours; for the townsman, the car to cocoon him in summer heat as he moves on winter missions through the tundra; for the reindeer-herding Lapp and the winter sportsman, the snow-mobile or motorized toboggan. Domestic air services have been the ultimate means of binding Nordkalotten to the rest of Scandinavia and are probably the most important single factor inducing change in the north.

In a way, all new techniques such as these, together with the new organizational methods that accompany them, are relatively more important for Nordkalotten than for other parts of Scandinavia. At the same time, partly because of the extensiveness of the area and its general backwardness, their effects have been more delayed and more circumscribed than in the south. In the process of their diffusion, some of the old problems have been solved and some eased. Inevitably, solutions to old difficulties have brought new problems in train.

The principle of comparative disadvantage

The Scandinavians place increasing stress on the principle of comparative advantage when engaging in domestic and inter-Scandinavian planning. It is most economic for each area to produce the goods for which its ratio of advantage is greatest and its ratio of disadvantage least as compared with other areas. They are correspondingly sensitive to the situation of Nordkalotten in this context. From the human, economic, and political points of view it suffers comparative disadvantages and in them its manifold problems are rooted. The particular emphasis manifested by each type of problem differs somewhat from country to country. The urge to tackle Nordkalotten's problems collectively waxes and wanes in response to the pervasive and shifting political pattern at the international level. Norway, Sweden, and Finland are equally aware of the latent internal opportunities of their north country and equally apprehensive of the external constraints that inhibit its development. It is a situation which reflects the fact that for a full generation Nordkalotten has been an integral part of the world economy and polity. Its inhabitants, for better or for worse, are correspondingly conscious that they are now very much citizens of the world.

2 Social Problems

Nordkalotten has a population of some 935 000, divided as follows: Nordland, Troms, and Finnmark 460 000 (1970); Norrbotten, 260 000 (1969); Lappi 215 000 (1970). For comparative purposes it is worth noting that Murmansk *oblast* has well over half a million inhabitants, with some 250 000 in the city of Murmansk—far and away the largest urban concentration in the broader Calotte area. The attitudes and reactions of the inhabitants of Nordkalotten to contemporary economic and political situations are rooted in physical and historical circumstances. It cannot be claimed that all of the inhabitants have been born in the north country, but the great majority are native to it. Not infrequently those who move into Nordkalotten develop a stronger attachment to their adopted region than those whose families have lived there for generations. The immigrants certainly help to sharpen the regional feelings to which the indigenous people give only limited expression.

Physical circumstances represent a turn of the screw on all the familiar Scandinavian characteristics. H. L. Mencken's 'chilblained north' is even more chilblained in Nordkalotten. The consequences of this are traditionally accepted in the north and largely disregarded in the south. Historical circumstances in Nordkalotten differ considerably from those in the southern and metropolitan parts of the three States. In addition, it has had a delayed reaction to events which have stirred the south. Until the 1950s, Nordkalotten remained active pioneering country with land-winning as a feature of its daily life. Colonization continued to be encouraged in the provinces of Oulu and Lappi after the post-war resettlement of displaced Finns in order to attract a permanent labour force in and around Finland's State forests. Nordkalotten also remained subsistence country for longer than most other parts of Scandinavia—some of it famine country, too. Moreover, in Nordkalotten the Finnish, Norwegian, Swedish, and Russian settlers intruded upon the more primitive Lapp. His territory shrank as they advanced. It was a peaceful withdrawal.

Nordkalotten differs in other ways from the rest of Scandinavia. First, four languages and cultures meet and mingle in it—a fact inseparable from the ebb and flow of people within it. Next, the greater proportion of its land area is owned by the State. In 1542, Gustavus Vasa declared that all land in Sweden (including Finland) not privately owned was henceforth the property of the crown. Thereafter, settlement in this area was by permission of the crown. When Finland became an independent republic, most of Lappi became State-owned land—the State, in consequence, becoming one of the most extensive owners of forest land in Finland. Most of the fell country in north Norway is owned by the communes (local authorities).

'The Kingdom of Lapland'

It was through the Lapps (or *Sabme*, as they call themselves in Lappish) that Nordkalotten first made an impact on people outside Scandinavia. The name 'Lapland' was freely inscribed on sixteenth- and seventeenth-century maps, and the territory and its people were brought to the attention of Europeans through travellers' tales as well as through the cartographer's art. A considerable mythology developed about Lapps and their country. On some maps, Lapland emerged as a 'kingdom' in its own right. In fact, the Lapps never organized their territory and medieval Lapland was a political no-man's land intruded upon by Norwegian, Swede, and Muscovite tax-gatherers. Norway claimed the coastland as far as the White Sea, Russia then claimed it west to Lyngenfiord; Sweden claimed interior Finnmark pushing out to Altafiord. Olaus Magnus's splendid pictorial map of 1539 indicates two other emerging characteristics of Lapland—and they have foreshadowed features of the twentieth-century life of Nordkalotten. First, he represented Lapland as an area in which rivalries between Sweden-Finland and Muscovy were played out in military campaigning. Secondly, the vignettes on his map recall that Lapland was the missionary field of two rival churches—the Western (Roman Catholic and then Lutheran) and the Eastern (Russian Orthodox). The Lapps were only slowly wooed to Christianity, the Skolts, a minority group, yielding to the persuasions of the Orthodox Church. The reputation of the Lapps for wizardry, partly related to the hallucinations bred of dietary deficiencies or peculiarities, dies slowly.

Occupation of Lapland was by way of the

coasts and waterways. On the outer ocean, Norway and Russia slowly established their positions. The foundations of a fortress on Varangerfiord—Vardöhus—were laid by Håkon V. Magnusson in the early thirteenth century. The first Vardö church was established beside it in 1307. By the Neiden river, the Orthodox missionary Trifon established Russia's north-westernmost chapelry and named it after the princes Boris and Gleb. Eastwards, the Russians created their trading posts on the Pomorze or Pomorian coast—the coast of the Kola peninsula.

On the inner sea, Lapland was divided administratively into great marches or Lappmarks, each tied to the ports that were established at the mouths of Nordkalotten's rivers—Piteå, Luleå, Torneå, Kemijoki, Oulujoki. It was by way of these waterways that the Swedish and Finnish traders collected furs, and pioneers settled the Calotte, finding in its abundant fish and game generous compensation for farming risks. In 1751 a Lappmark boundary was defined, to the north and west of which a territory was reserved for the Lapps. Just over a century later, in 1867, Sweden defined a so-called *Odlingsgräns* (boundary of cultivation) to the north and west of which only limited settlement was permitted in the Lapp territory. In 1889 Russia introduced restrictions on the movement of Swedish and Norwegian Lapps into its grazing areas.

Poet and scientist alike brought Nordkalotten into the frame of European reference. At the same time as vicars were establishing their churches, colonists were penetrating the Calotte valleys and military surveyors were marking and mapping its political boundaries. The scientists included the French mathematician, P. L. M. de Maupertuis, who, in the company of Anders Celsius, determined the correct shape of the earth from observations made at the polar circle in the Torne valley 1736–7, and the Swedish polymath, Carl Linnaeus, whose robust narrative from his Lapland journey in 1737 acquired world renown. The French scientific expedition to the high north in 1838–9 included the artist Paul Gaimard whose paintings provided a new appreciation of the north Norwegian scene. Some of the parish priests who took to the wilderness wrote classics in their own right. Jacob Fellman's *Observations during my residence in Lapland*, published by his son in 1906, and Petrus Laestadius's *Journals*, from his missionary work in Lappmark in 1828–32, provide examples. Among the travellers whose narratives drew attention to Lapland were Edward Clark (1799), Joseph Acerbi (1799), A. F. Skjöldebrand (1801–2), Leopold von Buch (1807), and Arthur de Capell Brooke (1823). The travellers shared experiences with the countryfolk, recorded the ethnographic mingling of peoples, admired the brawn of the settlers who portaged upstream, and praised the skill of the pilots of the tar-carrying boats who shot the rapids downstream.

The Finns have been most freely and frequently involved in the mingling of peoples. They were active members of the Birkarlar (*Pirkkalaiset* in (Finnish) who established medieval trading connections between the coastlands of the inner sea and the outer ocean. Finns not only colonized a great lobe of land beyond the Torne river, but already by the end of the seventeenth century had crossed the narrows of the Gulf of Bothnia and were settling the interior Lappmark of Piteå. For Bjorn Collinder, Sweden's northernmost county is accordingly 'many-tongued Norrbotten'. The area of the *Finnbygd*, or Finnish settlement as the Swedes call it, is bounded approximately by the Kalix river to the west. It constitutes eleven parishes,* within each of which Finnish is the first language. Finnish has also been a significant language for the Norrbotten Lapps. It was the *lingua sacra* in which most of the missionary work was done.

North Norwegians were early to identify the Finns as *Kvener* (*Kainulaiset* in Finnish). The *Kvener*, attracted seawards by the seemingly more secure life of the Norwegian fiordlands, and pushed from the interior by marauding Muscovites, established a number of coastal settlements from the early eighteenth century onwards. The Russo–Swedish wars of the early and mid-eighteenth century encouraged Finnish movement to north Troms (Lyngen and Nordreisa), to Alta, to Börselv in Porsanger, and to Tana. The famine years of the 1860s caused further migrations to Varangerfiord. In the mid-nineteenth century, there were over 400 Finns in the copper centre at Kåfiord, while Vadsö (Vesi-saari, in the language of the immigrants) became the best-known *Kven* centre.

Finn, Muscovite, Swede, and Norwegian have all penetrated Lapp territory as settlers so that the Lapps are now a minority people in their historic homeland. Censuses identify rather more than 40 000 Lapps (25 000 in Norway, 10 000 in Sweden, 4000 in Finland and about 2000 in the U.S.S.R.). All save a few hundred of them live in Nordkalotten. They are usually identified as persons who have learned Lappish as their

---

* Parishes are ecclesiastical divisions, smaller and more numerous than the local government communes.

mother tongue. The Lapps are unique ethnographically, although only a minority pursue the traditional reindeer husbandry, the remainder engaging in fishing or simple cattle farming. Because of the intimacy of their adaptation to the natural environment, their way of life has been highly sensitive to intrusive influences. All around the edges of their society and economy there is evidence of submission—at best, of lowly compromise. The so-called Sea Lapps on the coast of Norway represent one form of compromise; the sedentary farming Lapps of the interior, another. Marrying with Norwegians and Finns, the Lapps frequently lose the best of both worlds, becoming castaways of both societies and economies. Today, probably not more than 2000 Lapps follow a minimum of 600 000 semi-domesticated reindeer; but nearer 10 000 are probably dependent on reindeer husbandry. Reindeer herds have rarely been larger, their market value never higher. Reindeer meat production in Finland alone is 2 million kg a year. In all three countries a considerable return on invested capital accrues to the national economy from reindeer.

After political boundaries in northern Scandinavia were formalized, the transhumant Lapps were given special passports in order that they might move freely across the frontiers that intercepted their reindeer routes. When Scandinavia became a common passport area, special permits were no longer needed. New types of physical obstruction such as roads have been drawn through their territory, however, and the Lapps have become victims of the revaluation of resources. A conflict of interest between two different systems of values has consequently arisen. Although most disagreements are local in incidence, the cumulative effect of a larger number can be considerable. To the extent that farming retreats from the reindeer territories, the historical friction between the nomad and the settler is reduced. Indemnification of farmers for damage caused by reindeer nevertheless remains and special funds are accumulated by the Reindeer Associations to meet this contingency. Large-scale reindeer grazing and trampling is very harmful to woodland, while insecticides and fertilizers used in re-afforestation programmes may be harmful to reindeer. Major hydro-electric power schemes such as those in Sweden's Lule valley and in Norway's Alta and Tyrfjord, come into conflict with old-established grazing rights. So, also, do extensive mineral workings. While new roads and established railways may help by providing access to herds, both are also to a certain extent obstructive, and may have to be fenced against reindeer. Different forms of use of the same resources stand in competition. Beyond all this, there is the problem of maintaining lichen pastures in the face of growing herds. Nordkalotten consequently has a problem of prior inhabitants whose rights and attitudes as first-comers must be respected, but who cannot be set apart from the other citizenry in reservations as museum specimens. The future of the Lapps presents Nordkalotten with a social problem unique in Western Europe. The problem acquires juridical overtones when the Lapp population constitutes the majority in a parish, such as Utsjoki. It is compounded when there are Lapps who for status or prestige reasons wish to return to reindeer husbandry.

For many Lapps, *genius loci* and *genius speciei* remain more important realities than community feeling. Nor are common sentiments easy to foster when there are many different Lapp groups speaking widely varying dialects and spread over extensive distances. Some Lapps are submerged by the features of modern living, some slavishly pursue them, relatively few are able to resist them. On the other hand, Norway, Finland, and Sweden suffer no dearth of enthusiasts and sympathizers to proclaim the Lapp nation. Pressure groups urge the establishment of a Lapp parliament, the multiplication of Lapp schools, radio programmes in Lappish, the refinement of the code of Lapp laws, and the transliteration of place names into Lappish, and they spring to action to plead the Lapp cause as occasion arises. One point is clear—a sound economy is the surest way of maintaining the distinctive culture of their scattered patriarchal communities. The Lapps constitute rather less than five per cent of the population of Nordkalotten. To keep their case in perspective is no easy task.

The distribution of population

Statistics suggest that Nordkalotten is underpopulated. Troms has 5·4 inhabitants per sq. km; Finnmark 1·6; Lappi 2·3; Norrbotten 2·8. Underpopulation is, however, a relative term. The distribution of population in Nordkalotten is very uneven. Kirk Stone regards all of the area as falling within his 'zone of discontinuous settlement'. From coast to interior the discontinuities become greater. Population has always concentrated principally on the coast. The coastlands of the outer ocean have been occupied for several millennia longer than those of the inner sea.

The impact of the modest number of inhabitants

is impressive because of its concentration. To journey along the Atlantic coast of Nordkalotten is to be surprised by the seemingly uninterrupted scatter of human settlement. The panorama that unfolds from the deck of the express steamer is rarely without its white wooden houses: so, too, the skein of the highway as it takes over the function of the railway beyond Fauska.

Bodö (28 500), Narvik (13 300), and Tromsö (38 100) make some claim to being regional cultural centres as well as service centres. The other largest municipalities in Norway's Nordkalotten are Hammerfest (7000), Kirkenes (Sør Varanger) (10 500), Mo i Rana (26 100), and Alta (11 000). Over 90 per cent of the population lives within 4 km of salt water. Back from the coast stretch the uninhabited *vidder*.

Norrbotten and Västerbotten have their principal settlements on or near to the coast. Luleå (58 900) is Norrbotten's administrative centre and the largest city in Nordkalotten. As with Umeå (56 100), capital of Västerbotten, it has an estuarine site. To the east is Haparanda commune (18 900) on the Finnish frontier: to the west, Boden commune (27 100), the chief Swedish military settlement in Nordkalotten. Southwards is the port of Piteå (32 000).

Across the Bothnian Gulf, Oulu (86 600) on the approaches to Nordkalotten is Finland's sixth city. Immediately to its north is Kemi (29 700). The 'capital of Finnish Lapland' is Rovaniemi (29 200) immediately south of the Arctic Circle and at a confluence site. The historic fur market town of Tornio has shrunk in importance. The two largest inland urban communes are Finland's north-easternmost paper and pulp settlement of Kemijarvi (6400) and Sweden's iron-mining commune of Kiruna (30 600).

Beyond the coast, with its intermittent ports and—as they call the fishing settlements in Norway—its *fiskevaer*, population is clustered in the loose agglomerations of several thousand inhabitants that constitute the administrative centres of the communes of Nordkalotten, the church villages that grew up in the historic parishes of the area, and the specialist industrial, mining, and hydro-electric settlements. A network of ecclesiastical parishes and communes evolved to meet the needs of expanding settlement, especially in the nineteenth century. It presumed a stability in distribution which is currently challenged. Rationalization of local government boundaries by Sweden in the 1960s has caused Norway and Finland to question the efficiency of a pattern of administrative units born of other times to meet other needs.

Royal Norwegian Embassy, London

Tromsö, one of the largest towns in north Norway, has added a lively summer tourist traffic to its traditional role as a point of departure of shipping to the Arctic

Population mobility springs from many causes and some of these will be analysed in the ensuing chapters. The relative equilibrium attained during the inter-war years was disrupted by the Second World War. Widespread German destruction in north Norway and north Finland resulted in the displacement of most inhabitants. Rehabilitation was generally completed by the mid-1950s, with most displaced people returning to the sites of their former homes and reluctant to relinquish them in favour of socially and economically more efficient groupings. So many of the resources of

Finnish Foreign Ministry
Rovaniemi, located at the confluence of the Kemi and Ounas rivers, was completely destroyed in 1944. The newly-built city is the administrative centre of the Finnish province of Lappi

Norway and Finland were absorbed by reconstruction and rehabilitation that they were left a decade behind Sweden in material progress. Thus, although the whole of Nordkalotten displays active population mobility, the background to it and character of it differ substantially from country to country.

Four types of mobility can be discerned: (1) retreat from the frontier of settlement with complementary migration to urban areas in Nordkalotten; (2) movement from Nordkalotten to other parts of Norway, Sweden, and Finland; (3) migration into the area; (4) old-established, large-scale, seasonal migration.

The retreat from the frontier began in Sweden. It preceded withdrawal in Norway and Finland principally because Sweden became a modern industrial state in advance of them. The retreat gathered momentum in the 1950s. Investigating the process in detail, Eric Bylund has observed first that all but four of Norrbotten's nineteen rural communes declined in population between 1950 and 1969; secondly, that migration away from their isolated interior areas was differential. Most of the migrants are young people: older members of the family tend to remain on the farmsteads and in the rural communities. As a result, age levels rise at the same time as population diminishes and the old-established dynasties of farmers are dying out. Furthermore, none of the counties of Nordkalotten displays the same degree of urbanization as the counties in the southern half of Sweden. The negative results of rural depopulation are consequently not significantly offset by the rise of healthy urban centres. The high birth-rate down to 1960 has been succeeded by a lower birth-rate which cannot compensate for population outflow. Prognoses of population in Norrbotten down to 1980 suggest that at best the province will retain its existing population; at worst, that there will be a decline by more than one-fifth to 190 000.

The time lag, in high latitudes, of Finnish and Norwegian population developments is evident also in demographic structures. Although the birth-rate in Lappi provinces has steadily declined since it achieved a Finnish record in 1948, it still exceeds those for all other Finnish counties as well as for complementary parts of Norway and Sweden. Rovaniemi displayed a birth-rate of 25 per cent in the early 1960s—the highest for any Finnish city. The death-rate has declined steadily and is now below the average for Finland. Lappi county has accordingly a much higher rate of natural increase than Finland at large. In addition to its youthful characteristics, Lappi population has a higher proportion of males than of females—a traditional frontier characteristic.

In north Norway, the demographic features display a progressive deterioration from Nordland, through Troms to Finnmark. Indeed, demographically speaking, some parts of interior Finnmark were, until the 1950s, more characteristic of the nineteenth than of the twentieth century. For example, infant mortality in Finnmark exceeded 50 per cent down to 1950—and still remains near to 30 per cent. Together with much of Lappi, Finnmark also has a high proportion of young people: 40 per cent under 16 in 1970. At the same time life expectancy in north Norway is lower than that for the rest of the country.

The migration to urban areas is partly, but not entirely, related to the retreat from the rural frontier. In north Norway, for example, the growth of the urban centres is fed more by the movement of population from the agglomerated rural settlements than from the farmsteads. In Lappi county, the natural increase is so great that the urban population has increased whilst rural population numbers have been sustained.

Nordkalotten loses large numbers of emigrants to the south so that its counties show a relative decline of population in the national picture. Since 1950, for example, proportionate to the population of Norway as a whole, Finnmark has lost 7 per cent, Troms 5 per cent, and Nordland 6 per cent. This loss is more frequently from urban or agglomerated areas than from rural areas and is often composed of the younger, more energetic and skilled elements. It is inseparable from the general tendency for migration to increase as the numbers engaged in the service and manufacturing sector increase.

One of the most striking features of the pattern of migration since 1965 has been the strongly varying movement from Finland into Sweden. There has always been a modest migration from Lappi to the adjacent Swedish province of Norrbotten but the end of the 1960s witnessed a dramatic increase. In 1969, 3·6 per cent of the population of Lappi province crossed the border. Among explanations are the real or presumed fact that in Sweden wages are higher, jobs more secure, houses more easily obtained. The more vigorous promotion of industry in north Sweden also contrasted with the prolonged Finnish policy of colonization of the north. Young Finns from farming communities have responded increasingly to the potentially contrasting opportunities. Population loss from north Finland has called into being a Finnish Government Commission the task of which is to inquire into the reasons for the outflow. Predictions forecast that the population of Lappi is likely to be 25 000 less in A.D. 2000 than in 1970.

The permanent population of Nordkalotten has been stirred for centuries by seasonal migrations. Although their numbers may have dwindled proportionately to those of former times, their presence still makes its own particular contribution to the population picture. The merchants, whose summer portages were described in such detail by Olof Burman nearly 400 years ago, have become salesmen. But the ebb and flow of fishermen which predates recorded history continues. In the past they have moved overland from the anchorages of Russia to the 'summer-coast' or north shore of Kola, from interior Finland to Arctic Norway, and along the Inner Lead of western Norway. A climax is still encountered in the Lofoten fishery where thousands of vessels engage in the cod harvest during January to March. There is a second, though lesser, crescendo of activity in response to the summer cod fisheries off the north Norwegian coast. Life along the littoral responds accordingly—the fish racks bend with the weight of drying cod; the deft fingers of fishwives (Finnish as well as Norwegian) trim interminable fillets for the deep freeze; the fish oil, fish meal, and fish fertilizer factories belch out their noxious

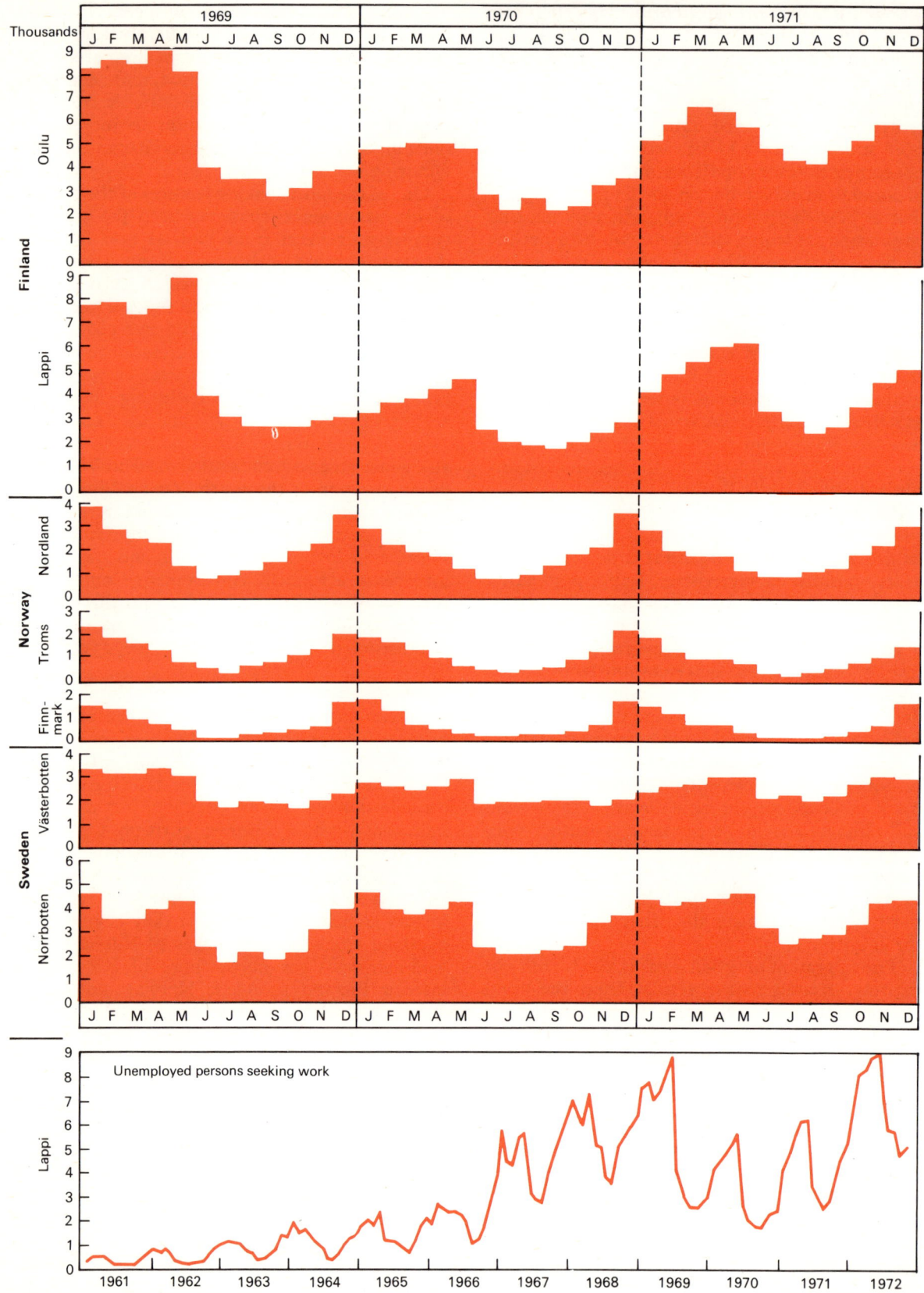

odours. Mobile services move in—first-aid ships, vessels to generate supplementary electricity, mission ships, cinema ships, tourist ships. And as has been the case for centuries, they are soon accompanied by pedlars, confidence tricksters, and all the others who sniff out a surfeit of ready cash.

The ebb and flow of lumberjacks to the northern forests of Sweden and Finland belongs essentially to the twentieth century. They have hitherto penetrated only marginally into Nordkalotten, but since the late 1950s all the forested areas of Scandinavia have been brought within the compass of commercial felling. In the process, however, the casual labourer has been replaced by the skilled operator, the solitary lumber camps have been supplemented by migratory caravan sites, horses complemented by fleets of tractors and lorries. And the entire operation is conducted according to the letters of many labour laws. Whereas in former times there were large-scale movements into Nordkalotten from the south, most movement today is short-distance from within Lappi and Norrbotten themselves. Furthermore, the timber floater—that hero of much popular Scandinavian literature—is also in process of elimination. Along river valleys such as that of Kalixälv, the percentage of timber moved by water has fallen by 50 per cent in thirty years.

Unemployment and under-employment, long-term and seasonal, lie behind much of the mobility. Fig. 3 gives some idea of the rhythms of unemployment for the northernmost areas of Nordkalotten during recent years. It must be remembered that these areas are occupied by communities all of which have compulsory military service (which removes considerable labour from the market). The figures are for the registered unemployed—not for those who are looking for additional employment. They conceal the age structure of the unemployed, most of whom are over fifty. This higher age category also contains considerable numbers of people who lack specialist training, who are not easily retrained, and who eventually become unemployable. It has been of the nature of the northlanders that they have known how to do a little of everything and nothing to the full—*aliquid in omnibus et nihil in toto*, was the way Petrus Laestadius expressed it.

Finally, Nordkalotten has always known an element of vagabondage and such men share in it. The classical literary illustrations of this are the Nordlanders August and Edevart of Knut Hamsun's novel *Vagabonds*. Wandering in search of a fortune which they never find, they represent the rootless and shiftless minority that lives around the edges of the hyperborean communities. August 'had never been discharged from a job, but had left each place of his own free will, had each time merely given in to his wanderlust, his desire to be moving on'. Escapism is undoubtedly an important cause of mobility in the population of Nordkalotten.

Fig. 3. Rhythms of unemployment in northern Scandinavia. The statistics, supplied in each case by the relevant Ministry of Labour, are not strictly comparable from country to country; but they illustrate general trends. For Norway, they refer to 'Persons registered at the Employment and Seamen's Offices'; for Sweden, 'Unemployed registered at the Employment Offices'; for Finland, 'Unemployed Persons seeking work at the Employment Offices' (in Rovaniemi and Oulu administrative districts the boundaries of which approximate to but are not precisely coincident with Lappi and Oulu counties). The lower diagram illustrates the development of the seasonal rhythm of unemployment in Rovaniemi administrative district since 1961

3 Economic Problems

In a world context—and to a large extent in the context of Europe—the Scandinavian countries are regarded as affluent lands with a high standard of living. But a high standard is far from uniform throughout their areas. In general, Norway, Sweden, and Finland display a steady diminution of wealth and opportunity from south to north. The variety of resources contracts, renewable resources are restored more slowly, climatic hazards increase, and the distribution of opportunity becomes more sporadic. This physical deprivation is exaggerated by the remoteness and extensiveness of Nordkalotten. Remoteness imposes its tax on exports to and imports from European markets and it restricts association with metropolitan Norway, Sweden, and Finland. Extensive distances within Nordkalotten have their own inhibiting effects.

The distinguishing features of the economy of Nordkalotten are rooted in these facts. First, it is in so many ways territory at the margin of the Scandinavian economy. It is not the only marginal territory in Scandinavia, but a larger part of the surface area of its counties lies outside

Fig. 4 The principal resources of Nordkalotten

Based partly on F. Isachsen and H. Myklebost, *Fabritius Verdensatlas* (Oslo, 1972) and on *Landsdelsplan for Nord-Norge* (Oslo, 1972). Place names to which reference is made in this section may be found in the *Atlas of Sweden*, the *Atlas of Finland*, and the Norwegian maps in *Fabritius Verdensatlas*

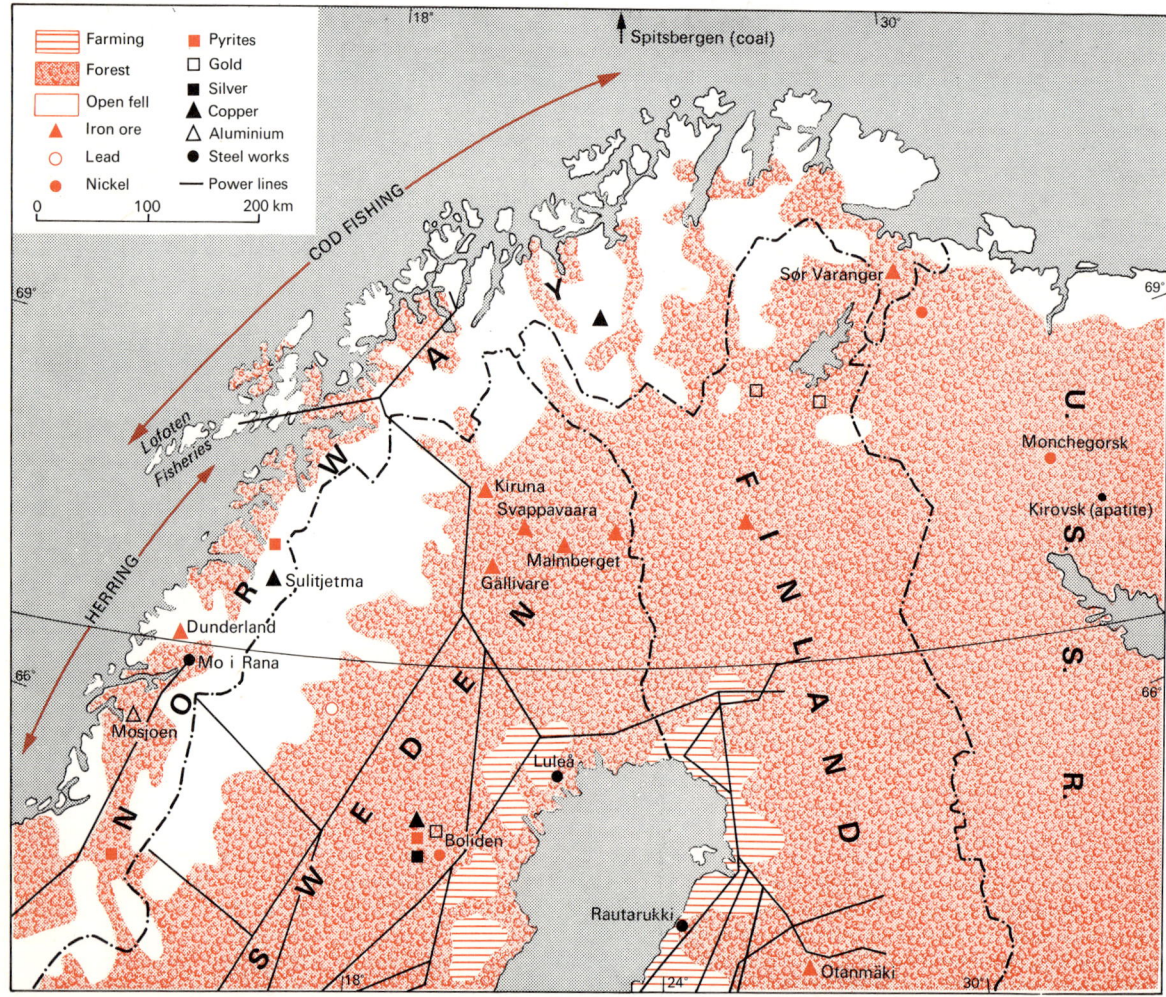

Northern Norway has an increasing number of trawlers similar to this 300-ton vessel, which operates with a crew of twelve and delivers an annual catch of 1800–2000 tons

the permanently settled and economically employed territory than that in any other part of Norway, Sweden, and Finland. Secondly, it is dependent territory—and its people are increasingly conscious of its dependence. It is dependent on outside markets for the disposal of its primary products and on outside sources of supply for most essentials of modern living. In addition, it is traditionally dependent upon the rest of Scandinavia to organize its economy and has become increasingly dependent on the rest of Scandinavia to sustain it. Decisions concerning its organization are made principally in the metropolitan areas of the south. This is natural for what in the third place is largely—though by no means entirely—under-developed country. The capacity of Nordkalotten for capital accumulation is limited. Development consequently depends more upon what is injected from without than upon what is saved within. Fourthly, an under-developed economy such as that of Nordkalotten lacks the flexibility of a fully developed economy. And restraints on manoeuvrability imposed by physical setting are an additional brake on attempts to improve flexibility. Finally, with people thin upon the ground, human interaction is less intense. The sum of human experiences is correspondingly less varied and one might say that the quality of life is reduced.

The nature of the raw materials

Nordkalotten may have less wealth per square kilometre than most parts of Scandinavia, but it has a relatively high potential for development. Its wealth lies principally in minerals, timber, fish, and water power. With the exception of the fisheries, most of Nordkalotten's natural resources are under-developed; accordingly commercial use of them has been delayed until the philosophy of conservation has been widely accepted. The agricultural resources of the area are undeniable, though in the context of the mid-twentieth century, they suffer organizational problems.

Fisheries

The inshore and offshore fisheries of Nordkalotten's oceanic waters are among the richest in the world. Preservation of its fishing rights was one of the most sensitive items on the agenda of Norway's negotiations with the E.E.C. The principal argument for excluding other fishing fleets is the lack of alternative employment for many north Norwegians. The situation is most critical in the counties of Nordkalotten, where 10 000 are employed exclusively in fishing with many others for whom the pursuit is part-time. North Norwegians are also disturbed by the intrusion of the larger and better equipped trawlers that move in seasonally from south Norway. Forebodings about the decline of Norway's fisheries are regularly expressed. Cyclical fluctuations in the harvest of the sea and the periodic shift of the fish-runs still defy explanation by the scientist. Overfishing is difficult to define. The salmon rivers of Nordkalotten, legendary to nineteenth-century fishermen, settings of local disputes and of litigation between those on their upper and lower reaches, still yield well—those on the Atlantic slope better than those on the Baltic slope. The increasing population of seals in the Gulf of Bothnia probably explains the difference as much as any other fact, and raises sensitive ecological problems.

Forests

Nordkalotten's Baltic slope has extensive forests. Qualitatively they are inferior to those of most of Sweden and Finland, the spruce petering out before the ultimate timber limit that is defined by the pine. Conifers take twice as long to mature in Nordkalotten as in south-central Scandinavia. So, too, do the increasingly valuable birch trees. The monetary value of forest land per hectare in Norrbotten or Lappi is less than a quarter of the value per hectare in south-central Sweden or south Finland. The State is the principal owner, though in Finland extensive areas of woodlands were made over to resettled farmers in the post-war years. Moreover the degree of dependence on the forest lot increases northwards in Finland and Sweden, so that the size of farm-holdings needs to be larger than in the south. In the Finnish counties of Lappi and Oulu fully three-quarters of the farm income derives from the woodland.

In Nordkalotten, farmer-owned timberlands are not usually as well-managed as State-owned forests. Because of the extent and unbroken character of their woodlands, the State Forestry Boards are in a stronger position to employ the economies of large-scale production and long-term planning than elsewhere in Scandinavia. They are also able to engage in extensive experiments. For example, poor quality woodlands have been widely cut over and burnt over in order to speed regeneration of improved stands through seeding. The harvesting of seeds from high-quality parent trees is a specialist pursuit in its own right. Drainage as a means of increasing timber increment is more important in Nordkalotten than in other parts because of the higher proportion of boglands.

Although the pursuit of forestry is less economic in Nordkalotten than most parts of Scandinavia, it has acquired increasing favour over farming since the middle 1960s. Farmers in Nordkalotten have to adjust to a general Scandinavian situation in which there is an excess of farm products and a potential deficit of timber.

Minerals

The mineral deposits of Nordkalotten represent pockets of wealth which contrast with the surrounding wastelands. The deposits are unevenly distributed, unevenly investigated, and unevenly exploited. Small-scale mining in Nordkalotten has a 300-year history. In the eighteenth century the iron ore of Malmberget was transported by reindeer sledge to coastal smelters. In 1826 British entrepreneurs acquired rights to mine copper at Kåfiord in Alta. Indeed, the Kåfiord smelting plant was the first significant industrial establishment in Nordkalotten. In the 1850s British mining engineers obtained concessions for the iron ores of Dunderland in Nordland. They also made the first attempt to transform operations in the Gällivare area in the 1860s. In size and output, the Kiruna mine dominates absolutely. It is located in the fell country, above the tree line and nearer Narvik than Luleå. The ore body—4 km in length, 90 m broad, and 2 km deep—has a 60 per cent iron content. Annual production is 16 million tons. Tuollavaara, a small adjacent mine, produces 1 million tons annually. Output from the Gällivare–Malmberget area, which is closer to Luleå, is 5 million tons. The most recently opened site is Svappavaara, 50 km to the south-east of Gällivare. It yields 4 million tons per annum. Laisvall, in Norrbotten's fell country, is the site of Europe's largest lead mine, opened in 1943.

By comparison with Sweden's resources, those of the Norwegian and Finnish sectors of the Calotte are modest. Finnmark has Norway's largest iron ore deposit at Sør Varanger, adjacent to the old settlement of Kirkenes. Its low-grade ores have been worked since 1906, but the operations were transformed by the addition of a pelletization plant in 1952. Concentrates exceeding 2 million tons are exported annually. Copper pyrites is produced at Sulitjelma, near Bodö, and there is also copper mining at Repparfiord in Finnmark. Lead and zinc are produced in Bleikvassli in Nordland.

Mineral sites in north Finland are restricted in size and number and are mostly marginal to the Calotte area. Iron ore is produced at Raajärvi in Kemi Valley and Kolari in Torni Valley. In 1934, the Mond Nickel Company, a subsidiary of the International Nickel Company of Canada, was given the right to develop the Petsamo nickel field. Installations were begun at Kolosjoki, and from 1941 onwards the German authorities tried to bring them under the control of I.G. Farbenindustrie. The smelters were destroyed in 1944 and the concession was compulsorily purchased by the U.S.S.R. when the Petsamo corridor reverted to the U.S.S.R. following the peace settlement in September of that year. Finland

Kiruna, northern Scandinavia's largest iron-mining centre, has a population of *c.* 30 000

thereby lost one of its most valuable sources of mineral wealth and western Europe its principal nickel deposit. Nikkeli (*c.* 20 000), the Russian community now tributary to the Kolosjoki mine with its electric furnaces, is linked by rail to Murmansk.

The mineral deposits of Nordkalotten are the lively concern of mining engineers. Improved survey methods speed the preparation of a mineralogical map. Less well known is the detail of discovery and development in the Russian sector of Nordkalotten. Between the head of the Gulf of Kandalaks and Murmansk, along the axis of the Murmansk railway, large-scale mining settlements have mushroomed. Among them are the planned communities of Kirovsk (*c.* 46 000),
with nearby apatite mining, and Monchegorsk (*c.* 50 000), with nickel production. Such sites encourage the hopes of investigators on the Scandinavian side of the border, though their value for the U.S.S.R. raises issues of strategy and defence.

Hydro-electric power

The flow of untapped energy remains proportionately higher in Nordkalotten than in any other part of Scandinavia, but the proportion of potential energy in the north country differs from State to State. By comparison with those of western Norway, the resources of most of the Norwegian Calotte area are limited. Altitudes are lower and precipitation is less than in west

Norway. The head of water and volume of flow are correspondingly smaller. North Norway only produces about 12 per cent of the national total of electrical energy, with Nordland absolutely the richest province.

North Finland, by contrast, claims the country's principal source of water power. The Kemi river system lies almost entirely in the Finnish county of Lappi. Although its basin experiences a low precipitation it has greater altitudinal variations than any other Finnish river basin. Not surprisingly, it has been the principal concern of Finnish hydro-electric engineers for a generation. As with Norrbotten's rivers, its water-power sites call for dams. The first large-scale construction, at Isohaara near the Kemi estuary, was completed in 1949. Twelve out of the thirty planned stations are completed. In order to make the maximum use of a seasonally irregular flow, Kemijärvi—one of the two largest lakes in Lappi province—has been regulated. In addition, two extensive artificial lakes are being constructed on the upper reaches of the system—at Lokka reservoir and Porttipahta. Reports have also been produced on the potential of the rivers originating in the Kuusamo area.

The Lule river basin in the Swedish sector of the Calotte is one of the largest and most impressive on the Baltic slope. It is richer in energy than any other Swedish river system. The installations at Porjus, Harsprånget, and Ligga represent the largest single developments in the eastern face of Nordkalotten. To them have more recently been added those of Leitsi and Seitevare on the Lilla Lule river and Vietas on the upper reaches of the Lule river proper.

The integration of the Scandinavian power grids proceeds slowly. Both Sweden and Finland have national systems. There are now high tension links across the Torni border between Kalix (Sweden) and Ossauskoski (Finland), Letsi (Sweden) and Petajakoski (Finland). Norway lacks a national grid, so that its Calotte systems operate independently of other national networks, but the Ofoten and Lyngen power systems are linked with the Swedish power grid. There is also a link between east Finnmark and Petchenga in the U.S.S.R. recently completed.

So far, no joint Scandinavian enterprises have been initiated on any of the Calotte's border rivers, though both the Torne (shared by Sweden and Finland) and the Tana (shared by Finland and Norway) have considerable potential. Proposals to divert the outlet of Sweden's lake Torneträsk to the Norwegian coast, thus capitalizing on the high head of water, have foundered on the problem of maintaining an adequate discharge in the river valley and the opposition of conservationists. Curiously enough, the most impressive cooperative schemes have been with the U.S.S.R.—the Pasvik stations jointly with Norway, the Tuloma stations with Finland. Potential for the production of hydro-electric power in Nordkalotten at large greatly exceeds potential consumption. Accordingly, additional production is essentially for export to the south.

Farming

Almost all forms of agriculture are precarious in Nordkalotten. Nevertheless, farming is widely distributed. Subsistence agriculture has been a common and critical feature for the area until within living memory and, when external sources of supply have been interrupted or reduced, its importance has been intermittently restored. Animal husbandry, with cattle dominant, has always taken precedence. The grazing season is reduced to a minimum in sub-Arctic Scandinavia: the period of indoor feeding reaches a maximum of eight months. Accordingly, fodder crops are essential. During the inter-war years, the accumulated results of biological research began to make their influence felt and agriculturalists were able to map a striking poleward march in the frontiers of cropping. For example, spring wheat was harvested both in Kemi and Torni valleys. Much more important, ley farming was extended and intensified to complement the fodder supplies of the meadowlands. Hay crops now occupy fully three-quarters of the field area in Nordkalotten. But improved land is lost in the wilderness of unimproved countryside. Finnmark has only 0.15 per cent improved land.

In general, commercial farming is not an economic proposition in northern Scandinavia. Combined with forestry or fishing (or both) farming provides a useful complementary activity. But Scandinavians have realized increasingly that the biological possibilities of much agricultural activity have stepped beyond the economic limits of production. It is important to remember that the same broad developments that have facilitated agricultural advance in the north of the country have favoured even more the intensification of farming in the south. In any case, the south is favoured over the north because the principal consuming markets are on its doorstep. There is a double paradox. Firstly, at a time when the physical possibilities of farming in the high north of Scandinavia were never better, the economic opportunities have been increasingly restricted. Secondly, in a period when maximum flexibility

Harsprånget power dam on Lule river in the Swedish province of Norrbotten. The associated underground power station is one of a chain of plants along Sweden's greatest source of energy. The power plants are State-owned

Swedish Embassy, London

is called for in farm structure and operation, farm operators have been slow to make adjustments in their practices. Farming, an almost unavoidable casualty of material progress throughout most of Scandinavia, is absolutely vulnerable in Nordkalotten. And, because it is in the nature of diffusion that the north is the last part of Scandinavia to react to external impulses, the farming communities are suffering the more because of the delayed response.

The organizational framework

It will be evident that the economy of Nordkalotten is more loosely strung together than that of most parts of Scandinavia. The units of administration are larger and the networks of communication are more thinly meshed than elsewhere. It follows from the smaller number and more dispersed nature of farm holdings, of concentrations of rural population, and of towns and cities than in southern Scandinavia, that organizational structures which have proved successful in the south are not necessarily suited to the north.

This is a fact immediately evident at the level of the individual farm-holding. It is estimated that to be a viable proposition, a farm unit in north Scandinavia must be larger than in the south. An economic unit should probably combine 20–50 hectares of cultivated land with 100–300 hectares of forest land. Most farms in Nordkalotten are well below the optimum size. Indeed, farms of a theoretically viable size are exceptional. In Lappi county, for example, there are only just over one hundred farms with a

Pyhätunturi is typical of the watershed country of sub-Arctic Finland. It is located at the tree-line and its farming settlements are on Europe's frontiers of cultivation

cultivated area exceeding twenty hectares. Furthermore, profitability is inseparable from location, and the great majority of north Scandinavian farms are detached holdings frequently standing in considerable isolation from neighbours.

At the community level, the means of identifying the minimum size for an effective settlement are increasingly refined. It is possible without difficulty to calculate the relevant population number for each function. Investigations in both Norway and Sweden have shown that it is difficult to support basic social services such as schools, health centres, and old people's homes, or commercial services such as banks and co-operative stores (let alone a State-owned liquor store) in settlements of less than 2500 inhabitants. Moreover, with the need for a minimum population growth of 4 per cent per annum to sustain the status quo of services in such communities, the prospective situation presents an increasingly acute problem. In all three countries, a comparison of the proportion of the population living in agglomerated settlements of two or three thousand shows the number to be smaller in the north than in the south. In Norway, for example, it is only 40 per cent by comparison with 60 per cent in the south. Such settlements tend to be increasingly deprived as services become increasingly specialized and expensive. Beyond all this, there is the population threshold for the commune itself. Working in the Finnish context, Mauri Palomäki urges that it should be 8000 and only in exceptional circumstances should a commune with less than 4000 inhabitants retain its legal functions.

The problem of the central place is even more acute. It is estimated that to support a full range of urban services a minimum of 30 000 inhabitants is needed. Nordkalotten has hardly a handful of towns that approach let alone surpass this figure, although the catchment area of a town may tip the balance. Beyond all this, Nordkalotten has no regional capital—strong national feelings would operate against the theoretical city of 100 000 inhabitants that might do much to provide a focus for the area. Only Oulu is within striking distance of such a figure and its location is very peripheral. County planners in Norrbotten see the quadrilateral area defined by Luleå, Piteå, Älfsbyn, and Boden (with nearly 130 000 inhabitants) as a possible substitute for a simple regional centre.

While the problems of organization are increasingly appreciated by the inhabitants of Nordkalotten, there is often resistance to organizational change. New adjustments in the north are largely reactions to impulses coming from the south. Economy and society in the north do not always react in the same way as in the south. Organizational structures which are successful in the south do not always fit circumstances in the north. Systems of values are not always the same in Nordkalotten as in the metropolitan parts of Norway, Sweden, and Finland. Mental attitudes are certainly different.

4 Political Problems

A third group of problems has political roots. Problems which lend themselves to a politico-geographical interpretation may be divided into those springing from internal stresses and those born of external pressures. Internal stresses are largely the consequence of centrifugal forces, with distance from the centre of authority encouraging opposition, and partly the result of ethnographic facts. External pressures are a product of international relations, which Nordkalotten experiences in its own distinctive way.

Internal considerations

Mental attitudes

Changes in population mobility, distribution, and structure are closely related to changing mental attitudes. In the past, the attitudes that have prompted mobility have been inseparable from food shortage and under-nourishment. Food deficiency has been virtually eliminated, though local dietary shortcomings remain. There is no denying that the availability of medical services is poorer in Nordkalotten than in other parts of Scandinavia and that standards of health are lower. While little scientific evidence exists to prove that the unusual daylight–darkness rhythms of Nordkalotten affect behaviour, tensions have a habit of building up during the dark period and 'dark sickness' is still an acknowledged winter ailment. *Mens morbida in corpore sano* is an aphorism which has been applied to the people of Scandinavia's high latitudes, though statistics do not support the popular opinion that the suicide rate is higher, that the incidence of violent deaths is greater, or that alcoholism is more frequent than in southern Scandinavia. In so far as impressions are correct, perhaps the inbreeding resulting from small, hitherto largely closed communities has been more important than climatic features in explaining mental disturbances and physical disabilities.

Nor can science explain the personal qualities attributed to the people of Nordkalotten. In her novel *Hitom Himeln* (*Beyond Heaven*), Stina Aronson ascribed a natural taciturnity to the people of north Sweden, for whom 'speaking becomes an extravaganza, even a frivolity'. It would be equally appropriate to interpret this quality as an innate shyness. On the other hand, religious attendance and voting behaviour both suggest that attitudes are inclined to run to extremes. Pietism claims strong support in the north—Laestadianism (named after the nineteenth-century revivalist) is the form adopted by many Finns and Lapps.

The voting behaviour of Scandinavians has been more fully subjected to scrutiny by geographers than that of most peoples. In all studies, the component parts of Nordkalotten display a disproportionately large left-wing vote. In 1954, for example, the Swedish county of Norrbotten recorded a 21·4 per cent communist vote—higher than that of any other Swedish county. A number of communes in Norrbotten recorded communist votes of 30 to 60 per cent. The communist poll is similarly high in the Finnish sector of Nordkalotten, which some political observers have called 'the red quarter' of Finland. In the elections of 1957 and 1961 Finnmark had the largest percentage of communist votes of any Norwegian county. Alta commune took the lead with 28 per cent and Sør Varanger followed. That the figures for Norway are somewhat lower than those for Sweden and Finland is related to the resources of the sea which have encouraged individual initiative and guaranteed at least modest contact with the south.

The growth of the communist vote in Nordkalotten has its roots in facts of geography. Isolation is one cause—isolation of one settlement from another as well as of the area at large. A second cause is that Nordkalotten has remained for longer than any other part of Scandinavia a territory of primary industry. Its economy has been more earthbound. Manual labour, frequently unskilled, has taken precedence over other forms of activity. Partly for this reason, it is a countryside of economic insecurity. Market fluctuations are transmitted most swiftly to workers in the primary sector. The resultant unemployment and insecurity have bred mobility and restlessness. Historically, the mobility associated with the lumbering camps and the disruption of family and community life during the felling season have been related causes. These conditions bred the so-called 'forest communists' as distinct from the 'industrial communists'. The historical tradition also differs from country to country. It is more deeply rooted in Finland than in Sweden and

Norway. Finland's crofting struggle and its civil war of 1917–18, left such strong impressions that communism has persisted as a family tradition into the third generation. These are much more important than geographical propinquity to the U.S.S.R. which must not be exaggerated as a cause. Finns from Lappi and Oulu counties moving into north Sweden have carried the doctrinaire Finnish brand of communism across the border.

The radical mood is inseparable from the attitude of the periphery to the centre. While southerners look upon the Calotte as the subsidized quarter of their respective realms and resent the imposition of taxes that go to sustain it, many northerners regard the south as exploiting the resources of the north for the profit of the metropolitan areas. The concept of the 'vampire' saw-mill illustrates the attitude. Southerners are regarded as absentee landlords, whether they be executives of commercial organizations or the representatives of the State. Accordingly, there is suspicion of any attempt to introduce new controls from the centre and resentment of schemes calculated to change established ways of life—even if for the benefit of the inhabitants.

Ethnographic issues

There are two prevailing ethnographic problems —one Finnish, one Lappish. It has already been noted (p. 17) that one of the most distinctive features of recent migrations in Nordkalotten has been the movement of Finns into Sweden. Finns have been scattered over much of Nordkalotten for many centuries, but the scale on which they are spilling into Sweden is a new phenomenon. There is no ethnographic parallel to it elsewhere in Scandinavia. The Finns moving from Lappi to Norbotten across the Torne boundary enter a thinly peopled territory where they add to the old-established minority. In 1970, more than one-quarter of the population of Norrbotten were Finnish-speaking. While ethnographic boundaries in Nordkalotten at large are increasingly blurred in the process, ethnographic differences at the individual level are sharpened.

The principal cause of social stress has been and remains linguistic. In the late nineteenth century considerable concern developed at the inadequacy of teaching in the Finnish language. By 1900, only one-tenth of the Finnish-speaking Swedes were being taught in Finnish and by 1920 teaching in Finnish had disappeared. The last Confirmation instruction in Finnish was given in 1916. Yet in some areas of activity Finnish was indispensable. In courts of law, either bilingual (or trilingual, where Lappish was concerned) officials were necessary or interpreters had to be employed.

Solutions to the situation had to be found for two reasons. First, the Finnish minority became increasingly articulate and sensitive about its language. Secondly, the issue was taken up in the newly independent State of Finland, where the more extreme national elements had conceived the idea of a more extended Finnish State (*Suur-Suomi*) coincident with the boundaries of the Finnish language. It was not difficult to point to the widespread distribution of Finnish place-names in Norrbotten to substantiate historical claims. A formal glossary of them has been compiled for the Finnish place-name archive. Where there are major settlements, the Finnish forms for them are used in Finnish atlases, school texts, and official publications. Some of them are old-established, such as Ruija for Finnmark, Lulaja for Luleå, Tromsaa for Tromsö (Fig. 5). In response to this situation, more liberal Swedish opinion claimed that it was better to re-establish teaching in Finnish than to risk the possibility of ideas about greater Finland developing among the Finnish minority.

The striking increase in the Finnish population in north Sweden since 1965 has exaggerated the need both for teaching in Finnish and for the teaching of the Finnish language in northern Sweden. Newspapers have pointed the way by including Finnish language columns. Strictly speaking, the position of the immigrant population in Sweden is quite different from that of the resident Finnish population. The problem of communication is an accepted risk in a change of work-place and residence. Theoretically, Finland is a bilingual country, with Swedish as a part of the school curriculum. But Swedish is not readily spoken by the majority of Finns and the counties of Lappi and Oulu, principal recruiting grounds for emigrants to the western Calotte, are almost exclusively Finnish-speaking. Today, while only Swedish remains the official language west of the Finnish border, Finnish-language facilities are increasingly widespread. Recruitment of Finnish-speaking teachers is the problem. There are some 200 today in northern Sweden: the need is for 400–500. Even immigrant teachers are not forthcoming.

The Lappish situation slowly improves with the broadening acceptance of ethnic pluralism. The problem has subtle manifestations, the details of which have been investigated by Harold Eidheim in Norway. Because of ethnic intermixture it is not always easy to distinguish

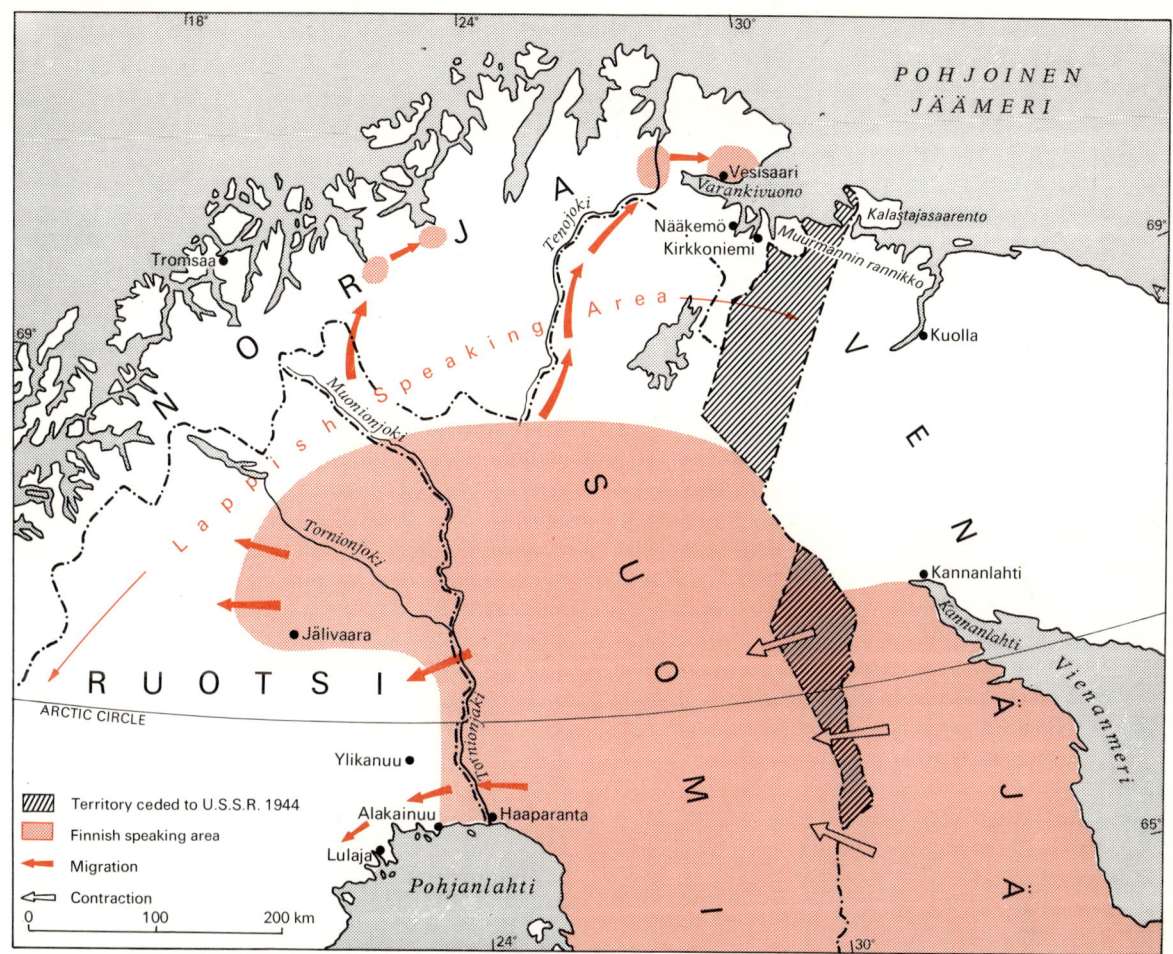

Fig. 5. Areas of Finnish-speaking settlement. Finnish place-names are employed on this map which also shows the area of formerly predominantly Finnish settlement in the U.S.S.R.

Lapps and non-Lapps in north Norway (in any case, many Lapps are 'Finns' in Norwegian terminology). Nevertheless there has been—and indeed remains—something of a social stigma attached to the Lapp. It is only disappearing as echoes of the earlier policy of Norwegianization disappear.

The features of a common technology may slowly extend over all Nordkalotten; the organizations of the Nordic Council may encompass in common institutions the tripartite territory, but there remain powerful residues of national feeling. In the case of Finns and Lapps these are exaggerated by the isolating fact of language, by different social practices and not infrequently by different physical appearances. The study of all these features is a happy hunting ground for ethnographers and anthropologists. But in day-to-day life assimilation in the host society is slow and many minor conflicts occur in personal and community relations as a result. Only among children whose nonsense verses display a splendid disregard for language differences is the problem momentarily resolved.

These internal stresses and strains are luxuries in which the three northern countries can indulge as long as their territories are suspended in a state of international equilibrium. But Nordkalotten is also a sensitive area internationally and in it Norway, Sweden, and Finland are confronted by a set of broader politico-geographical problems which call for constant compromises and adjustments. These compromises are represented in part by a framework of boundaries agreed and confirmed through the last two centuries. They express themselves in the form of political pressures which have broadened from the regional, through the continental to the world scale.

External considerations

Boundaries in Nordkalotten

The boundaries of Scandinavia's Nordkalotten are identified on Fig. 2. Their identification is an integral part of the political history of Scandinavia. The boundary between Norway (then a part of Denmark), and Sweden was formally staked out between 1752 and 1766. In 1815, Norway and Sweden were united in a dual monarchy and the Russo–Swedish boundary of 1809, stretching along the Torni and Muonio rivers was confirmed. It was a boundary which broke up a system of parishes previously united by and focused on the river. During 1825–6, a Russo–Swedish commission drew the boundaries between the two countries in the Calotte area. These were inherited as the western frontiers of Finland in 1917 when the Grand Duchy achieved independent status. In 1920, by the Treaty of Tartu (Dorpat), Finland acquired a long sought-for outlet to the Arctic Ocean in the Petsamo corridor, through which it constructed a 500-kilometre Arctic highway to the small port of Liinahamari (Fig. 6). This territory was ceded to the U.S.S.R. by the peace settlement of 1944, so that Norway again marched beside Russia. Surveyors of the two wartime allies had the interesting experience of formally plotting the boundary midway along the course of the Pasvik River. The Russian boundary also advanced westwards in the Salla and Kuusamo area of north-east Oulu county. The outlines of Finland's sector of Nordkalotten were confirmed by the peace treaty with the U.S.S.R. in 1947.

The strategic situation of Nordkalotten

By the end of the eighteenth century, the realms of Sweden–Finland and Denmark–Norway had declined in strength and influence in the European hierarchy of States. They were no longer controlling, but controlled. By the end of the nineteenth century, the Scandinavian countries had been reduced to a trio of small States sandwiched between three great powers, while on the far Atlantic horizon, a fourth great power was already affecting their lives and livelihood.

The situation was summarized by the Swedish political geographer Rudolf Kjellén at the time of the First World War. He saw Sweden—and by implication Scandinavia—as lying between two contrasting groups of powers. Russia and Germany on the continental front were military powers: Britain—and beyond it the U.S.A.—on the oceanic front were maritime powers. The Scandinavian countries responded to the predominantly political pressures of the former and the predominantly commercial pressures of the latter.

In the mid-twentieth century, the Scandinavian countries are still sensitive to the system of equilibrium established between their eastern and western neighbours, but the degree of stability or instability is now a response to a

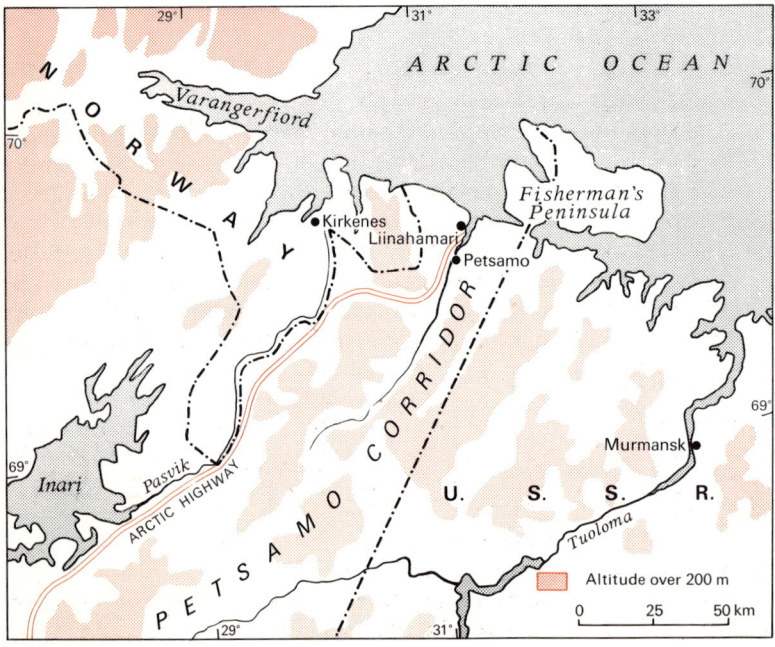

Fig. 6. The Petsamo Corridor. Finland's inter-war outlet to the Arctic Ocean was agreed by the Treaty of Tartu, 1920. An Arctic highway was constructed from Rovaniemi to Liinahamari on the Petsamo coast. The corridor reverted to the U.S.S.R. in 1944

world situation rather than to a set of regional circumstances. For these countries the U.S.S.R. and the U.S.A., with their associated alliances, are the principal controlling forces.

Each stage in this evolving situation has had its own particular effects for Nordkalotten, and the consequences have tended to differ for each of the three sectors. Accordingly, Nordkalotten's framework of political boundaries deepened the rifts within an area which stands more than any other part of Norden to benefit most from common policies and a common development.

For Nordkalotten, Russia is the most apparent external source of pressure. In reality or in imagination, the shadow of Russian aspirations has hung over Nordkalotten for two centuries. It is an expression of what the early nineteenth-century Swedish historian E. G. Geijer called Russia's 'yearning for the sea'. With the transformation of Russia into a major Baltic power after 1809 and the subsequent growth of its navy, there emerged the idea that Russia needed ice-free harbours and that the natural area in which to seek them was the coast of north Norway. Among residents who responded to the vulnerability of Nordkalotten was J. R. Crowe, a founder of the Kåfiord copper plant, a businessman with a knowledge of Russian and British vice-consul in Hammerfest. Between 1836 and 1855, Vice-Consul Crowe sent a series of dispatches to the British Foreign Office, apprising Lord Palmerston of the multiplication of Russian trading vessels engaged in the so-called Pomorze trade along the Arctic coast. Hammerfest alone received 150 a year. During the Crimean War, Britain signed a secret treaty with Sweden–Norway (1855), while Scandinavian political historians were already declaring that the watch-towers of Scandinavia should look to the White Sea and not to the Elbe or the Eider.

The idea of a Russian threat to northern Scandinavia was exaggerated by the development of railway lines in the high north. The railways of the Grand Duchy were constructed on the same broad gauge as those of Imperial Russia, so that the penetration of Finnish State Railways to the Torne river was regarded with apprehension. One observer spoke of 'a race of steam horses' on either side of the Gulf of Bothnia with the northland as the prize. Sweden, not wishing to compromise its international position, allowed the concession to the North of Europe Railway Company for the construction of a line from the head of the Bothnian Gulf to Narvik to lapse in 1888. Sweden's coastal line was extended to Boden in 1894, where public pressure led to the establishment of a military outpost. It was only in very slow stages that the line was extended eastwards to reach Haparanda by 1913. Meanwhile, Sven Hedin, the eminent Swedish explorer of Asia, pamphleteered on the dangers posed by Russia to Sweden by its concern for ice-free harbours at the approaches to the Arctic basin, and Rudolf Kjellén, the political geographer, urged the construction of an inland railway on the piedmont which was less exposed to possible assault from the east than the coastal route. Meanwhile, too, Russia began its Murmansk railway (completed 1915–16) and the conversion of its Arctic terminal from a fishing harbour to a naval base.

There was a second consideration of a politico-geographical character which affected railway development in Norrbotten—the allegiance of the Finnish-speaking community. Eventually, the railhead was pushed up the Torne Valley to Karungi (prestige necessitated a parallel Finnish line on the left bank). It was described as a psychologically important life-line and a cultural link with the south. But Swedo–Finnish stress was generated even by the naming of the stations. Not until 1931 was a decision reached by the Railway Board which had to strike a balance between old-established non-Swedish names and somewhat inappropriate purely Swedish names.

In the high north the shadow of the U.S.S.R. has succeeded to that of Imperial Russia. British anxiety for the security of the area was already expressed in 1918–19 in the Murmansk Campaign. Concern increased in the inter-war years with the growing dependence of the British steel industry on the north Swedish orefields as a source of supply. They were an important source for Germany also. Nordkalotten narrowly escaped direct international confrontation in early 1940 when Britain and France planned to send military relief to Finland by way of Narvik and at the same time to interrupt the flow of north Swedish iron ore to Germany.

During the Second World War the latent implications of the location of Nordkalotten were realized for the first time. Norway was occupied by German troops. Finland was engaged in hostilities with the U.S.S.R. and though not allied to Germany, was a co-belligerent. Sweden thrust the great bulk of Norrbotten county between much of divergent Norway and Finland. While German troops moved through this ostensibly neutral territory on their differing missions east and west, British and French commandoes raided targets on the Atlantic coast of Nordkalotten and Allied convoys braved the hazards of the northern sea route to Murmansk and the White Sea ports. In the process, they demonstrated for a future generation of Russians both the importance of these high latitude bases and their vulnerability to assault.

The full implications for Nordkalotten of the disruption of equilibrium in the system of external pressures were witnessed in the last months of the Second World War. In Finnmark and Troms, German troops retreated westwards before the advancing Russian army. In Lappi county, they retreated northwards before Finnish troops who were required by the Russian armistice terms of 1944 to purge their country of Germans. As a result of the German scorched earth policy, Finnmark, Lappi, and most of Troms experienced complete destruction of all property and means of communication. Even the Lapps had their reindeer slaughtered.

The war years gave rise to much economic and social distress in the Finnish and Norwegian counties of Nordkalotten. Priority in both countries was given to their rehabilitation. But although settlements and communications rose speedily from the ashes, they represented investment in reconstruction rather than in new development. Accordingly, by comparison with the Swedish sector, the Finnish and Norwegian parts of Nordkalotten suffered the loss of a full decade's progress. For north Finland, the war had another consequence—it gave rise to a minor stream of refugees from the severed eastern parishes of Salla and Kuusamo. Finally, if visible testimony is needed to remind the inhabitants that strategy has tugged Nordkalotten into European history, it exists in their extensive military cemeteries. In them the Allies of the eastern and western fronts are buried beside the Germans and the cosmopolitan casualties of their labour and prisoner-of-war camps.

The experiences of the Second World War have left the U.S.S.R. with heightened concern for the northern approaches. Murmansk has emerged as one of its largest naval harbours, a garrison city for marines, and possibly the principal Russian submarine base.

And at the same time as the U.S.S.R. intensifies its activities in Arctic waters from Murmansk and Archangel a new feature has appeared on the north Norwegian horizon to offer new opportunities and create new problems. The continental shelf off Nordkalotten's coast is a promising area of oil and natural gas deposits. Any attempts to exploit discoveries will create three problems. First, since in some eyes the Russian navy has already converted the Norwegian Sea into a *mare sovieticum*, any exploitation by Norway of the continental shelf north of 70° might be deemed to hamper the unhindered access of Russian naval vessels to the outer ocean from the Arctic basin. Secondly, oil drilling installations might well interfere with the operation of Russian underwater detection schemes. Thirdly, there are likely problems of interpretation in international law. Perhaps the approach to resource and sovereignty in Antarctica provides a model for the Arctic.

Norway, Sweden, and Finland have also had to adjust themselves to the strategic transformation of Nordkalotten in the light of the development of inter-continental ballistic missiles. The globe has acquired new significance for military authorities as well as in the schoolrooms of Lapland. In the 1960s Nordkalotten found itself athwart a new line of fire between the New World and the Old. Since then, the importance of fixed sites has diminished and Nordkalotten is no longer on the critical threshold for launching installations. The next stage in mental adjustment for the Norwegians is to accept the expansion of a missile-carrying submarine fleet on its Arctic doorstep.

Nordkalotten has resources. The task is to mobilize them and thereby to convert an unstable economy into a stable one. An unstable economy has led to an unstable society. The technical means for correcting the economic situation are available, but they are not always employed because the financial returns on investment are commonly less in the north than in the south. In basic economic terms, output per unit of input is lower. Despite this, Nordkalotten has never known greater material security than today nor have its inhabitants been so conscious of what Gunnar Myrdal has called the 'cumulative causation' that is responsible for it. Moreover, the social consequences of investment, though not capable of measurement, are probably higher in Nordkalotten than in most parts of Scandinavia. Improved material security is directly related to new-found accessibility. Unfortunately, the conversion of inaccessibility into accessibility has intensified the strategic significance of Nordkalotten. As a result, military insecurity has replaced material insecurity as the shadow hanging over the high north.

5 The Search for Solutions

The search for solutions to the manifold problems of Nordkalotten has taken place in the political framework of three different States, each of which has different policies at the international level. In turn, these policies represent the legacy of past allegiances and compromises. Since the policies are inseparable from Great Power relations, there is some logic in looking first at the solutions that the three countries have sought to problems arising from their international setting. Secondly, all three States have realized that it is impossible to deal with all parts of their extended realms as though they were areas of equal opportunity. Each makes special provisions within its nationwide legislation to ease the chronic problems of Nordkalotten. Though the problems may be much the same from country to country and the solutions adopted may have common features, the total situations differ considerably. In so far as there is stability at the international level, co-ordination in the application of common solutions across the borders of the three countries is eased.

Political solutions

The solutions to problems of political security represent the interpretations of three sovereign countries of the compromise position most likely to guarantee their territorial integrity and independence. They are not reached regardless of Scandinavian discussion, but they do not represent Scandinavian consensus.

Since 1815, Sweden has followed a neutral line. It escaped military involvement in both World Wars and aims at non-alignment in the international arena. Consequently, Sweden's part of Nordkalotten, though strongly fortified, has no external commitments. In accordance with its principles, Sweden has sought to reduce to a minimum foreign control over any enterprises in Nordkalotten. This philosophy lay behind the final nationalization of the Lapland mines in 1957.

In 1948, Finland signed a Treaty of Peace and Friendship with the U.S.S.R. This was renewed in 1955 and 1970. In contrast to the reserved attitude of Sweden, Finland aspires to an active neutrality and has taken positive steps to try and promote East–West schemes for demilitarization. It is not a member of the Warsaw Pact, but it is undeniably in what politicians would formerly have called Russia's 'sphere of influence'. It is a buffer state.

When NATO came into being consequent upon Russia's post-war intrusion into Europe and the ensuing 'Cold War', Norway and Denmark were founder members. As a result of Norway's commitment to NATO, Finnmark and Troms have become the most militarily significant part of Scandinavia. NATO and the U.S.S.R. meet on the Pasvik river.

The consequence of this situation has been the differential militarization of Nordkalotten. There is only limited secrecy about military establishments in the Scandinavian sectors of Nordkalotten. In Norway the outward signs of defence are visible to all—military airfields, fell-top radar stations, fortified sites, arterial highways, the flow of army vehicles—simply because so much of the open wilderness reveals more than it conceals. Finland, its military forces controlled by the terms of the 1944 peace settlement, has few defences. The so-called 'iron curtain' itself—scarcely a line of defence—marks the eastern limits of Nordkalotten. A military zone three kilometres broad anticipates the tall posts that support the hundreds of miles of barbed wire fence that are the Finno–Russian boundary.

In the context of this military equilibrium, Nordkalotten is evolving its own conventions. For example, Norway has not permitted foreign troop manoeuvres in Finnmark. Nor will it allow the stock-piling of nuclear weapons. Norway and the U.S.S.R. have also agreed not to fly military aircraft in the vicinity of their common border, while NATO aircraft have agreed to keep to the west of longitude 24°E.

Economic solutions

Nordkalotten is under-developed country with chronic problems of unemployment and underemployment—especially of a seasonal character. By comparison with the rest of Scandinavia, the area has lower incomes and lower capital investment. In all three countries the last generation has witnessed massive programmes of capital investment in Nordkalotten. This has taken many forms. First there was the need for reconstruction

Norsk Jernverk A/S

The steel plant at Mo i Rana in Nordland is a State-sponsored project. It was the first of the large-scale metallurgical complexes to be opened in northern Scandinavia

and rehabilitation in north Norway and north Finland. This type of investment represented largely replacement of lost capital rather than injection of new. But a measure of reorganization accompanied reconstruction, so that the lands that had been laid waste emerged more efficient in the process. Rovaniemi, for example, was given a new plan at the hands of Finland's most distinguished architect, Alvar Aalto. New prefabricated buildings, perhaps less appealing to the eye, but certainly constructed for more comfortable living, spread over the landscape. Not surprisingly, there was frequent resistance to rationalization. In Finnmark and Troms, for example, attempts were made to rationalize local settlement patterns, but many insisted on returning to their old isolated communities rather than abandoning them in favour of more accessible, better planned and larger communities which would be provided with more amenities.

Secondly (and simultaneously with reconstruction in Norway and Finland) plans were conceived to strengthen the industrial base of Nordkalotten. This has been achieved through direct capital investment by the State as well as by a variety of schemes to encourage private and local government investment. The most impressive State investment has been in the steel plants of Mo i Rana (Nordland), Luleå (Norbotten) and Rautarukki (Oulu). A/S Norsk Jernverk at Mo i Rana, initiated by legislation in 1946, draws its ores from Syd-Varanger and Narvik, its coal from Spitzbergen as well as mainland Europe, and its electricity from nearby Rössåga, the largest hydro-electric installation in north Norway. The steel plant supports a community of approximately 10 000. Immediately to its south at Mosjøen have emerged a privately sponsored aluminium smelter and a nylon fabric factory.

The steel plant of Luleå, Norrbottens Järnverk, was founded in 1940 as a State enterprise and is Norrbotten's counterpart to Mo i Rana. The successor to an earlier mill in Luleå, it has made a substantial contribution to the economy of coastal Norrbotten. Its intended capacity is 1 500 000 tons annually. Rautarukki, near Raahe, is a younger and more southerly Finnish counterpart, State-sponsored through international loans. Each of these three enterprises has been a planned attempt to create a growth centre on the margins of Nordkalotten and to promote the indirect as well as direct diversification of opportunity. To a limited extent manufacturing industry has begun to respond in the Luleå–Piteå area, with the establishment of component plants of the automobile firm Scania-Vabis, of Atlas-Copco, and of L. M. Eriksson.

Other forms of direct capital investment are found in timber processing. In Sweden, AB Statens Skogindustrier has created major softwood plants at Kalix and Piteå; while Veitsiluoto softwood factory at Kemi is State-sponsored: so, too, is the softwood enterprise at Kemijärvi (1960) in eastern Lappi county. Although the Kemijärvi enterprise has not been a commercial success in its own right, it has had an important influence in establishing Kemijärvi as an independent growth centre with a gravitational pull successfully competing with that of Rovaniemi over a wide area. A contrasting form of investment is found in the 'education industry'. Both Sweden (in Umeå) and Finland (in Oulu) have discovered a useful means of creating employment opportunities through their new northern universities, technical colleges, and conference centres. Umeå with a growing labour force tributary to its 7000 students, is marginal to the Calotte area, but it provides an example for Norway to follow in Tromsö, site of the northernmost university in the world. Sweden has also agreed upon the dispersal of other research institutes to Nordkalotten—the Forestry Institute to Umeå and the Geological Survey to Luleå.

The construction and maintenance of communication systems makes a somewhat steadier call upon labour—from maintenance of roads (especially following the springtime thaw), electricity and telephone wires (especially following ice storms), to lighthouses and seamarks along the Norwegian coast (especially in the dark season). On the Baltic slope, the revaluation of timber lands has called for a closer network of forest roads as well as for the improvement of selected floatage ways—both State enterprises where the forests are State-owned. Finland remains a railway building country and this activity absorbs a limited amount of unskilled labour (as well as drawing to Nordkalotten a trickle of tourists who aspire to drive home a spike). Military installations and highways have also had multiplier effects on the local economy, calling into being a variety of small-scale servicing activities.

All of these enterprises have created a sustained demand for labour; but there is a third form of capital investment which, although financially more sound, nevertheless offers only restricted opportunities for unskilled workers. This characterizes exploitation of water power. True enough, development of a river system such as the Kemi, with a score of projected power stations and elaborate watershed reservoirs, is likely to require a labour supply for a considerable period. But, as has already been demonstrated by Swedish experience along the Lule river, the mobile settlements of several thousand constructional workers are succeeded as each unit plant is completed by a few score of highly skilled permanent residents. The same applies to the Finnish labour forces that were recruited to construct the power stations across the border in the Russian sector of the Calotte.

Solutions to the problem of seasonal unemployment or under-employment are both financial and organizational. Winter has traditionally closed a great range of enterprises. Modern techniques reduce winter's impact, but at a price. For example, along the north Bothnian coast, harbours are normally closed for approximately six months, and harbour employees have to be given other jobs. Technically, it is possible for ice-strengthened shipping assisted by modern ice-breakers to maintain links with such ports as Luleå, Piteå, Kemi, and Oulu throughout the winter. The financial costs of such operations relative to land transport costs are falling sharply, especially if the social benefits resulting from continuous winter operations are added to the accounting. Again, whereas constructional work used to come to a standstill in winter, modern building techniques, from swift-setting concrete to heating installations, enable work to continue. It is more socially beneficial to absorb the heavy additional costs through regional and seasonal subsidies than to pay unemployment benefits. In the Calotte area, support is given to contractors to construct public buildings such as schools, hospitals, bridges, and State-subsidized housing outside the summer season.

All three countries have their particular development policies. Common to each have been attempts to promote workshop and small-scale industries through cheaper interest rates on loans

Finnish Foreign Ministry

The icebreaker *Nord* operating in the Gulf of Bothnia. With the aid of icebreakers and ice-strengthened ships it is possible to keep north Swedish and Finnish harbours open throughout the winter, but the cost is prohibitively high

and various forms of tax relief. But the sources of support for enterprise in the private sectors have changed in a variety of ways since the initial introduction of schemes in the early 1950s. In Finland, for example, a Regional Development Fund came into being in 1971. This fund is used for subsidization of business enterprise including the tourist industry, fisheries, and fur-farming.

It favours: (1) medium-sized, labour-intensive industries; (2) export industries; (3) industries which provide substitutes for imports.

Norway has special tax regulations and loan systems for Nordkalotten. In 1952 and 1972, North Norway Plans were approved at the national level. Among the development areas are the Lofoten Islands; while among the so-called experimental centres are Alta in Finnmark and Skjervöy in Troms. During the last two decades, the proportion of loans and guaranteed funds allotted to the three northernmost counties has been higher than that accorded to any other group of counties in the country. Representative of this large-scale initiative is the chip-board mill at Sørreisa in Troms county.

In general, Sweden has been more radical than either Norway or Finland in its approach to development policies. Since 1963, investment resources have been available to encourage industry to locate in Norrbotten, while the Labour Market Board has been empowered to give local authorities permission to allocate funds to public works expenditures on industrial buildings in the northern development area. Sweden has been more concerned with encouraging new industry than with underwriting older and less efficient concerns. Finance for development has been partly derived from holding back a proportion of profits from the iron-mining industry. Sweden has also laid greater stress on retraining schemes and labour mobility than Norway or Finland.

Sweden has been in the vanguard of rationalization on the farming front. It has led the way in legislation to reduce the number of farm units, in encouraging the amalgamation of holdings, and—on the northern fringes of settlement—in reclothing unprofitable farmland with profitable forest. Against the background of surplus farm production—especially of dairy products—it has introduced legislation to reduce its cultivated land by at least 1 000 000 hectares by 1980. Simultaneously, Norrbotten county planning authorities estimate that those engaged in farming will

A few of Lapland's estimated 600 000 reindeer. Such concentrations can have a significant effect on vegetation as they graze their way across broad swathes of country

Finnish Foreign Ministry

Finnish Embassy, London
Ice-hole fishing, a winter sport

fall to 2500 in 1980 by comparison with 5800 in 1970. In 1969 Finland legislated for the reduction of its cultivated area by 90 000 hectares and its dairy herd by 40 000 annually between 1970 and 1975. It is essentially in Nordkalotten that this legislation makes its greatest relative impact.

It has already been noted in Chapter 2 that the Lapps are automatically caught up in the changes that affect the Calotte area. Solutions to their manifold problems are increasingly organizational. Reindeer herding, which is anything but a scientifically-managed enterprise, has considerable potential. But in the first instance reindeer numbers must be brought into harmony with the carrying capacity of the pastures. In Sweden, attempts have been made under the Reindeer Breeding Act of 1971 to reorganize the Lapp districts so that breeding can be undertaken collectively, shelter provided, predators controlled, and mortality in calving reduced. Another feature of rationalization within this framework of proposals is slaughtering at 3 or 4 years instead of 8 or 9 in order to increase the turnover of stock. It is hoped that through improved methods of management, it might also be possible to reduce the number of man-days spent on each reindeer from two to one. State-sponsored slaughter-houses at such places as Karasjokk and Kautokeino, and refrigerated transport of meat products have made for more efficient processing and marketing.

But, although the Lapps constitute no minority problem in northern Scandinavia, there are Lapp problems of another kind. For example, there are too many reindeer herders (even though only Lapps in the strict sense of the term are allowed to engage in this traditional activity), reindeer trespass is a livelier issue than ever, and Lapp fishing and hunting prerogatives are in constant dispute.

Both State and private investors look to the tourist industry as a means of increasing employment opportunities in the high north; but the season (or seasons, if the winter skiing season is included) is short, returns on investment are low, the maximum demand for labour occurs when unemployment and under-employment are at a minimum, and in any case, labour cannot be effectively drawn from the unskilled pool. Although at the peak period of tourism accommodation may be inadequate, in annual terms only two-fifths of the capacity is used. Multi-purpose accommodation is now increasingly favoured—especially residential schools which can become tourist hostels or youth hostels in vacations.

North Cape and the Lofotens, as well as some

of the bird cliffs with their millions of nesting birds, have been tourist magnets for a century, but most of Nordkalotten has made little impact on Baedeker, Cook, and other guides. Even today, roads, weather, and insects discourage return visits to these absolute frontier lands of European tourism. Yet for a discerning minority, Nordkalotten has the virtue of empty spaces, offers happy hunting grounds for expeditions, and provides untouched wildernesses for the new naturalists. The eagle still sails the sky, the lemming still swarms, the wolf still marauds. Estuarine, fiord, river, and lake fisheries are among the richest and least polluted in all Europe. There are well-managed game resources for those whose sport is with the rifle. Local exoticisms exert their particular appeals—from gold panning in Finland's Lemmenjoki to the ceremony of the bear hunt. Seasonal attractions are found in migratory birds, in berry picking, in the vivid autumn colours of the open fells—the red season, as it is described—and in the Lofoten fisheries, which reach their climax in March and draw increasing numbers to jerk their lines for cod from the decks of tourist vessels. Finally, Nordkalotten at large is already accumulating its own mythology. It is based on ethnographic sources such as those of Samuli Pauluharju no less than on fiction such as that of Robert Crottet. It is given visual expression in the work of the Swedish artist, Ossian Elgström, at once ethnographer and symbolist, whose landscapes and people give a new dimension to the north.

Some 900 000 vehicles cross the Swedish border annually between Haparanda and Karesuando, about 45 000 the Finnish–Norwegian border between Kilpisjärvi and Heiligskogen. Most of the tourists that they carry are Scandinavians, and among them Finns are usually most numerous. Nordkalotten has a treble appeal for Finns. First, they encounter in the Calotte area landscapes which are entirely different from those of the broad peneplain that provides the background to most of Finland's life. Secondly, an excursion to the Arctic seaboard serves to remind some of the corridor of land that they once owned to saltwater at Liinahamari. Thirdly, throughout history there have always been Finnic peoples on the Arctic seaboard. A trip to Ruija, as Finnmark is to the Finns, is a pilgrimage—something quite different in character and meaning from a journey to the north country for Swedes or Norwegians.

All three countries have established and are extending their national parks and conservation areas in Nordkalotten. The old-established Forest

Finnish Foreign Ministry

Lapporten, the Gateway of the Lapps, with the lake, Torneträsk, is representative of the rugged landscapes that the Scandinavians are setting aside as national parks and nature reserves in sub-Arctic Europe

Swedish Embassy, London

Riksgränsen, the border area between Norway and Sweden, on the railway between Narvik and Kiruna, is the site of tourist accommodation which offers skiing until early summer

Research Institutes aim to protect the woodlands at the limit of tree growth and to conserve for posterity tracts of primeval forest or *Urwald*, while the influential Tourist Associations of all three countries play vigorous conservationist roles. Sarek, Padjelanta, and Stora Sjöfallet, in Swedish Lapland, are Europe's three largest national parks. Sarek, creation of Axel Hamberg, is probably the best-understood high fell area in Scandinavia. Upper Pasvik is in process of becoming Finland's largest national park.

Winter sporting draws Finns north more than the other Scandinavians—again because of the contrasting nature of the terrain and its growing accessibility. It has led to a certain amount of investment in equipment such as chair lifts, reindeer sleighs, and snow scooters (forbidden over large areas of Norway and Sweden). Highland Norrbotten becomes a playground for Swedes at the springtime equinox—with a rash of ice-hole fishing on such a lake as Torneträsk to complement skiing.

It is not easy to assess the contribution of tourism to the economy of Nordkalotten. A recent detailed survey of Lappi province estimates that the returns from tourism somewhat exceed the total income from reindeer herding. In Norrbotten it cannot be less, and it is undoubtedly more in Nordland, Troms, and Finnmark. Such a comparison puts the tourist industry into perspective. Naturally, the industry contributes more than money. It pulls in people and ideas from the outer world, reducing the feeling of isolation in Nordkalotten and facilitating understanding of it among the southerners. At the same time, it introduces additional components into the problem of multiple land-use and can promote local dissatisfactions. Indeed, the point of view is increasingly expressed that tourism is as potentially destructive for Nordkalotten as it is constructive.

Administrative solutions

It has become increasingly apparent that organizational solutions to the problems of Nordkalotten are inseparable from forms of administration and national allegiance. While the basic problems may be empty space, isolation of settlements, and limitation of opportunity, the approach to all of them is inseparable from the fact that Nordkalotten is a multijurisdictional area. It is divided into three at the highest administrative level and its international boundaries define systems of control and related power structures which are deeply entrenched. Though there may be resistance to central authority, the inhabitants of Nordkalotten hold ultimate allegiance to Norway, Sweden, and Finland.

At the same time, Scandinavia is one of the few parts of the world where the beginnings of a supra-national authority are stirring. The increasing integration of the five Scandinavian States not only simplifies co-operation across international borders, but positively encourages it. No part of Norden stands to benefit more from this than Nordkalotten. The creation of a common Scandinavian passport area (1957), the establishment of a common labour market (1954) and the integration of Scandinavian national health schemes (1967) have taken place within the framework of the Nordic Council (1952), which Finland joined in 1955. At its assembly in 1962, members of the Council began to explore the possibilities of planning inter-Scandinavian industrial development and location. Plans were formally initiated by a resolution in 1966. Members of the Council, conscious of the problems of the north country, have also promoted a Nordkalotten Conference. This Conference, which has met regularly since 1962, consists principally of representatives of relevant provincial authorities from the three countries. Like its parent body, it puts forward resolutions for adoption by the relevant administrative authorities. As a body keeping an eye on central government policy it is also likely to be critical if investment is made in other areas when it could be made in the north. There are also regular meetings arranged independently to which the U.S.S.R. sends delegates as well as more specialized scientific collaboration with organizations in Murmansk Oblast.

The foundation of EFTA in 1959, which Finland joined as an associate member in 1961, eased the commercial problems; but the inhabitants of Nordkalotten view the prospect of the E.E.C. with apprehension. Some speak of 'the shadow of Rome' again hanging over the land. Their peace of mind is not helped by economists who speak of extensive areas of Norden possibly bearing the same relation to the E.E.C. as Norrbotten now bears to south Sweden.

Meanwhile, various proposals have been put forward for strengthening the forces that bind Nordkalotten together. One is for the reorganization of local government boundaries. It will be recalled that Sweden has led the way in providing a framework of communes which corresponds more closely to current and prospective population requirements, and that Norway and Finland are following suit. It is clear that for reasons of physical geography there are some areas where the groupings can be more efficiently arranged across international borders than within them. One way of facilitating the administration of such areas would be to convert them into some kind of federal district. In theory, both the Kiruna–Narvik area and the Torne valley lend themselves to this treatment (Fig. 7).

Little precise evidence concerning the comparative conditions in the economy and the attitudes of the communities on either side of the international boundary of Torne river existed until a survey supported by the Nordic Council was conducted in 1969–70. Its findings are critical for any prospective federal treatment of Tornedal. For those who occupy the riparian parishes, the river unites rather than divides. Traffic across its border is lively and personal contacts are close. The survey revealed that 97 per cent of the Finns in the frontier parishes made regular shopping expeditions to the Swedish side: 85 per cent of the Swedes to the Finnish side. Eighty per cent of those living in the Finnish parishes and 60 per cent of those living in the Swedish parishes had relations by marriage or blood on the other side of the border. Every fourth woman in Swedish Tornedal had been born in Finland and every third Swedish boy had a Finnish girlfriend. Living conditions were found to be generally poorer on the Finnish side than on the Swedish side, education facilities inferior and employment opportunities fewer. This contrast induced different attitudes to agriculture and to emigration in the Finnish parishes. While the Swedish farmer tended to idealize his holding, the Finn was likely to react with active frustration to his lot. In addition, economic uncertainties with their associated insecurity were appreciably greater for young Finns than for their Swedish counterparts. Traditional features in social structure and social behaviour were more persistent on the Finnish side of the border. Thus, differences between the generations were less pronounced than in the Swedish parishes, the division of labour between men and women was more clearly recognized, the status of the woman in the home and her

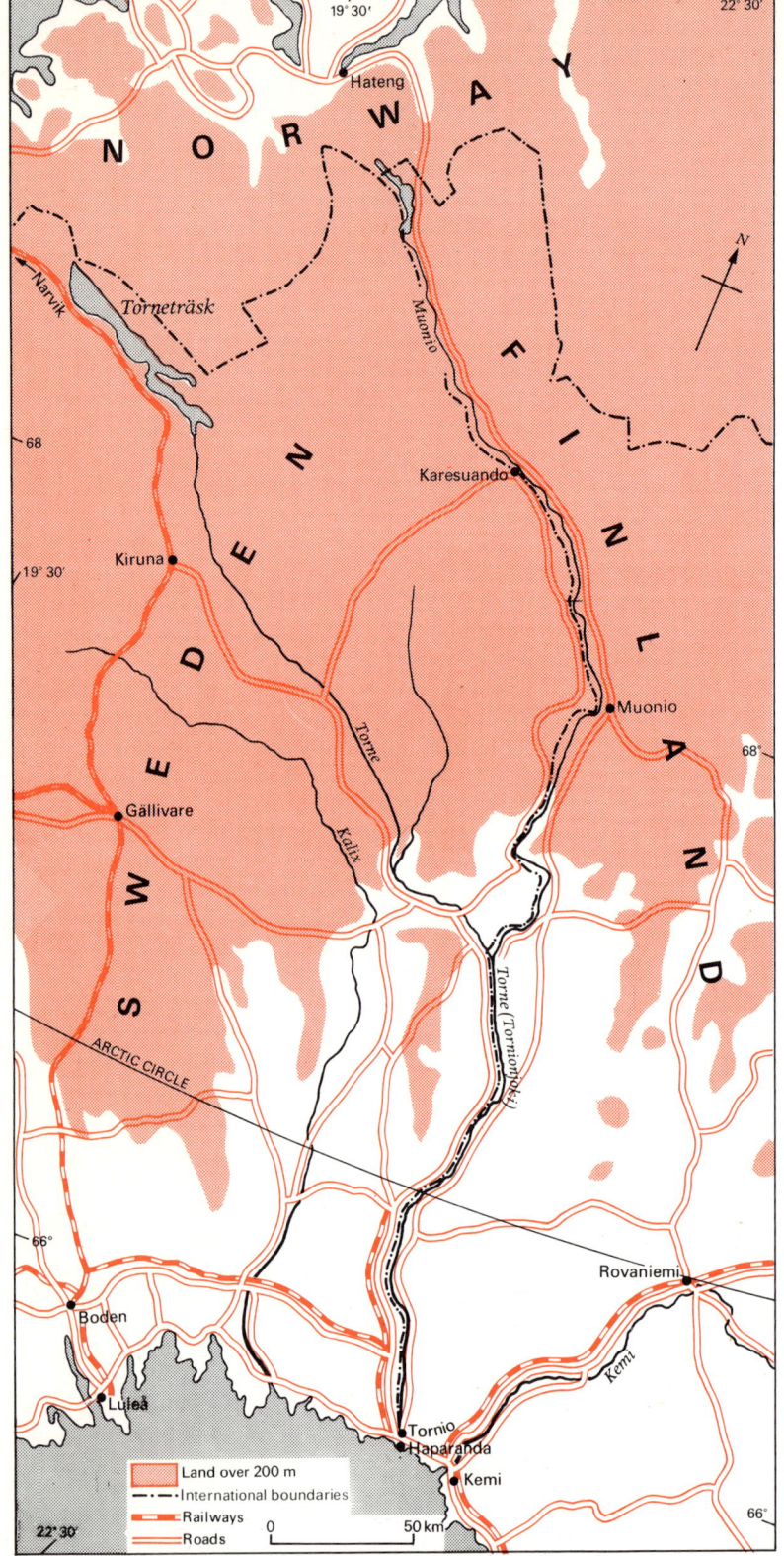

Fig. 7. The Torne–Muonio Corridor. This route is followed by the principal communications between the head of the Gulf of Bothnia and north Norway

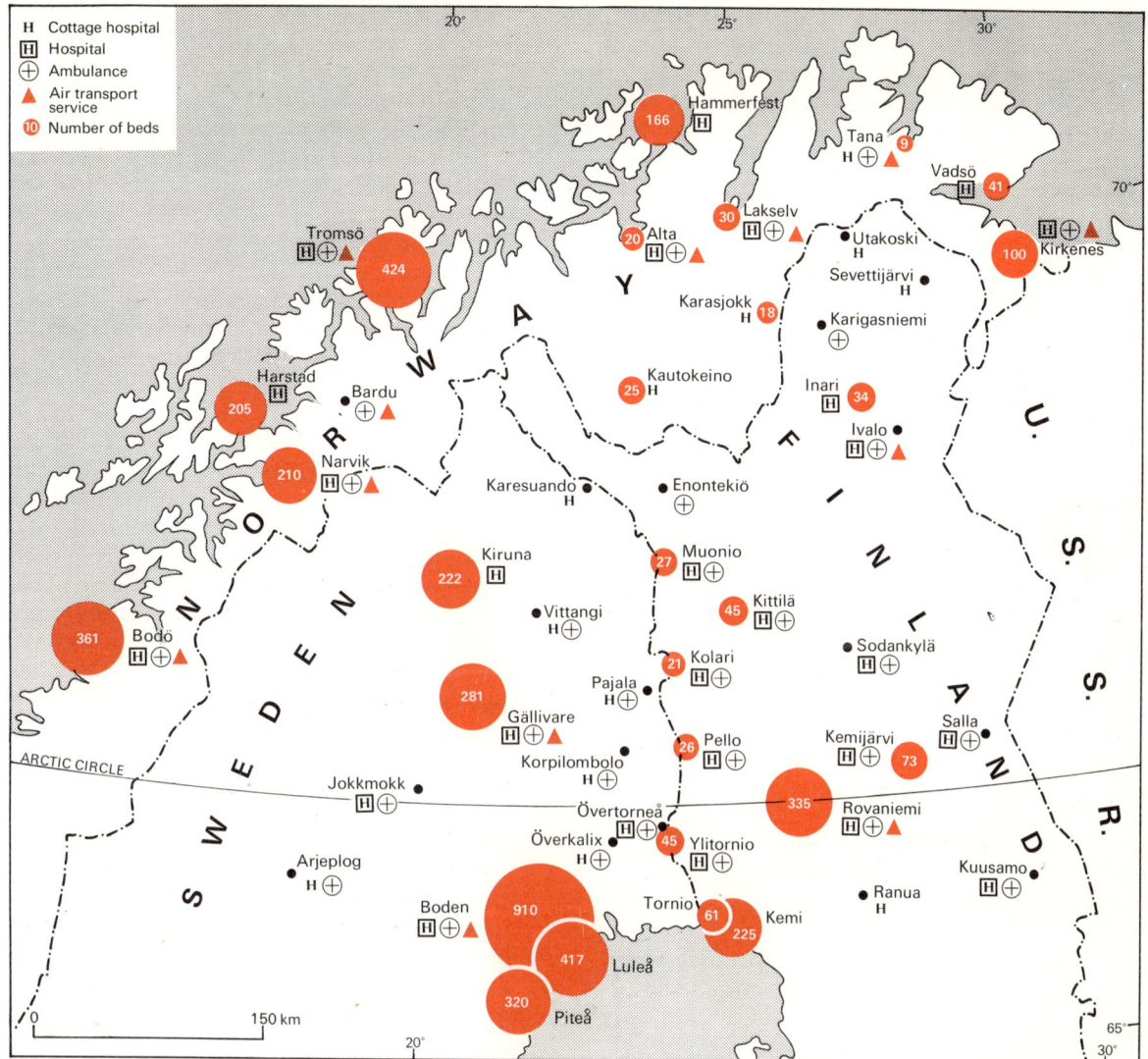

Fig. 8. Health services and related amenities in Nordkalotten

Based upon information in the report 'Samarbete om ambulanstjästen inom Nordkalotten', *Nordisk udredningsserie*, **11**, 1971 (Stockholm, 1972)

precise social position were more clearly defined. Pietist tendencies remained strong in the Finnish parishes, with Laestadianism claiming a continuingly powerful influence. This contrasted with limited church adherence and general religious indifference in the Swedish parishes. Among the 773 people questioned, most were very conscious of their position on the periphery of the State. Such detailed surveys are necessary to reveal the intimate ways in which differences are juxtaposed within Nordkalotten. They also indicate that there are unlikely to be any simple administrative solutions to the problems.

There are obvious areas where administrative cooperation across political boundaries can yield advantages. For example, practical steps have been taken in the field of hospital administration. Health services are thin upon the ground and, in the interests of economy of scale and professional efficiency, medical services have been regionally concentrated. A particular problem in Nordkalotten is the deficiency of ambulances. Fig. 8 gives some idea of their availability—in the province of Lappi they are almost all privately owned. Air ambulance services—using both light aircraft and helicopters—have proved highly important for coastal Norway. In all three countries military and police aircraft may be called upon to supplement these private services.

University administrators also step over international frontiers in Nordkalotten when planning and supporting academic research. Where there is limited finance, it is helpful to have agreed areas of specialization. The universities of Umeå, Oulu, and Tromsö operate joint programmes on Arctic medicine, biology, and archaeology, and they have established common field research stations. But the quickest way for an administrator to go from Tromsö to Umeå is via Oslo and Stockholm. A common Nordic institute for the promotion of Lapp Studies is also under way.

In order to attract administrators to Nordkalotten—or to encourage them to stay there—attempts are made at a financial level to adjust the amenity differential between north and south. Higher salaries have been paid for some time to many groups of people who work in the Calotte area. Norway's *Arktisk tillegg* (or Arctic subsidy), Sweden's *Kallorts tillägg* (literally, cold place subsidy), and Finland's rather more elaborately determined salary adjustments all take into account the need for extra fuel, the need for winter clothing, the inconvenience of having to travel several hundreds of kilometres on a return journey to the pharmacist, oculist, dentist, or library, and the transport costs that add to the price of many necessities. In addition, the provision of amenities is increasingly subsidized. Public libraries are of impressive size, swimming pools of Olympic dimensions, sports halls and covered shopping precincts of corresponding magnitude. The formulae for determining salary supplements, rooted in physical and economic geography and subject to regular review, are keenly watched by trade union officials responsible for the welfare of civil servants, local government officers, and professional bodies.

The illusion of logical structures

The search for solutions to the many problems that face the inhabitants of Nordkalotten is prompted by motives which range from compassion to guilt, from altruism to greed. But the basic concern is with inequalities of distribution in the natural world as they give rise to inequalities in human circumstance, and the basic fear is that regional disparities will become increasingly difficult to reduce. Regional imbalance is in many respects a concomitant of significant national growth in the Scandinavian countries: areas of development grow faster than areas which are under-developed. The object of most policies in the northlands is to multiply opportunities and to eliminate the shadow of subsistence, to reduce the friction of distance between Nordkalotten and its markets, and to ease and speed the provision of services and amenities to the inhabitants of this high latitude area. Another way of looking at these endeavours is to regard them as a search for logical structures to replace or to modify the existing and frequently illogical systems within which daily life operates. Those who promote the search encounter increasingly the prejudices of a population which is becoming steadily more articulate. They are finding that it is easier to construct technological and administrative frameworks that make for greater efficiency in the economy than it is to unravel the networks of tradition and belief that are at the roots of society. The success of the former is inseparable from an understanding of the latter. And planners are experienced enough to realize that technical change can make for economic deterioration as well as improvement, for new forms of instability as well as reduction of old uncertainties. In high latitudes, the recuperative powers of nature are slower than in lower latitudes. It is natural that the speed of adjustment of their old-established communities should also move at a slower pace than that of their counterparts in the metropolitan south. The harmonies and lazy rhythms of the *Gemeinschaft*—the rural community—are not easily replaced by the atonalities and faster tempos of the *Gesellschaft*—the industrial society.

6 The Way of the Four Winds

To summarize. Nordkalotten is emerging as a concept in its own right—in Scandinavia and in the broader European scene. Expressed in the simple terms of the classical economists it consists of: (1) a surfeit of land, mostly barren, set in a hard climate, remotely located from centres of supply and demand, occupied by (2) a thinly scattered population experiencing (3) a deficiency of capital, which has delayed technological progress, and (4) a shortage of managerial capacity, which is reflected in organizational shortcomings. The degree to which this imbalance is adjusted will be a reaction to the tug-of-war for supplies of (3) and (4). In turn, adjustments are inseparable from (5) the broader domestic policies of the three countries that share Nordkalotten and (6) international political considerations.

As the concept of Nordkalotten has emerged, the nature and degree of its problems have acquired heightened concern for Norway, Sweden, and Finland. In Nordkalotten some of Europe's most sophisticated societies are confronted with some of the least tamed parts of the European continent. The high north of Scandinavia and the adjacent U.S.S.R. remain frontier country in all senses of the word. Facing the icy wastes of the Arctic, the turbulent North Atlantic Ocean, or the limitless tundras of Soviet Siberia, they constitute outpost territories on which the absolute limits of many familiar ecological features of Europe are inscribed. For the anthropologist the pagan world is near enough in time to have left residual testimony; for the economist Nordkalotten is on the confines of the *oecumene*; for the militarist it is a new international marchland; for the tourist—according to his attitudes—Nordkalotten is a neglected recreational area on the circumference of a crowded continent or Scandinavia's counterpart to the Wild West.

Post-war technological development has been of greater consequence for Nordkalotten than for many areas—economically, socially, and strategically. This is for two reasons. First, it has helped to ease the physical strain of existence which, because of the harshness of the environment calls for a relatively more elaborate buffer between nature and man. Not until the means for creating this buffer had become economically possible could the new techniques be adopted. Secondly, although the pinched and perverse existence of many of Nordkalotten's inhabitants has been given a more rounded and relaxed character, it is only at the expense of their precipitation into the cut and thrust of the modern world. New interpretations of space and new distributions in space have resulted; but they have not called into being with equal speed more effective associations in that space.

This is because the unity of Nordkalotten is a chimera. Its identity is conceived largely from without. It is not, as yet, the product of any significant urge from within. The component parts of Nordkalotten lack the memories of a common history to draw them together. There is no homogeneous folk culture—and it takes more than collaboration between radio and television authorities to produce it. There is nothing approaching a common spirit and Nordkalotten has yet to demonstrate that, in the phrase of H. J. Mackinder, it is a 'going concern'. Feelings of sentiment exist in the high north, but at a lowlier level. The inhabitants of the Finnish province of Lappi, for example, have a much stronger attachment to Perä Pohjola (the Far North of the province) or to Länsi Pohja (West Northland) than to Lappi, let alone Nordkalotten. Where a sense of solidarity is expressed it is as likely to be in protest as in purposeful endeavour. It is easier to reduce the mystique of national boundaries and national sovereignty in Nordkalotten than to replace them with a new regional allegiance.

From what has been said, it may well appear that the peoples of northern Scandinavia, like Atlas, carry a world of woes on their shoulders; but all territories have their problems and the perception of them differs according to whether one is born to them or is viewing them clinically from the outside. Despite the hardships and tensions in Nordkalotten there are plenty of northerners whose innate attachment to their native plot or acquired involvement with its issues binds them closely to it. In addition, a growing number of southerners have developed an allegiance to the north: scientists who are drawn to its natural phenomena, conservationists who seek to protect the wilderness, recreationists who court the simple life, artists who endeavour to capture the northern scene in paint or fabric, men of letters who search for its fundamental

By courtesy of the Trustees, Norbottens Museum, Luleå

The Bear Feast a pen and ink drawing with water-colour wash by Ossian Elgström (1883–1950).
Elgström, an ethnologist as well as an artist, derived much inspiration for his robust pictorial narrative from the descriptions of Lapp life and customs by Swedish missionary priests who had worked in the high north during the eighteenth century. For Lutheran Sweden the heathen Lapps presented a moral problem. The bear was considered an almost sacred animal by the Lapps. Consequently the bear hunt was surrounded by ritual; the bear feast, by ceremonial. A wealth of topographic and ethnographic detail is crowded into Elgström's depiction of an event which was once a regular occurrence in Lapland. The bear hunt is still an isolated feature of life in the eastern parts of Nordkalotten; the bearskin, a coveted trophy; the very carefully prepared meat, a rare delicatessen

truths. Peter Dass blew the first trumpet for Norway's Nordland three hundred years ago. Jonas Lie gave to it new romance a century later. For Finland, Akseli Gallén-Kallela caught the nature of the sub-Arctic forests in his tortured and tormented pines and the poet Eino Leino the dialectic of darkness and light in his *Lapland Songs*. The Lapps themselves have given their own artistic interpretation of Nordkalotten—from Nils Nilsson Skum's primitive paintings to Johan Turi's diary of the annual round of the reindeer herder. Translation has made available to most Europeans *The Way of the Four Winds*, Yrjö Kokko's magical appreciation of Lapland.

There are many ways of looking at northern Scandinavia. Indeed, Kokko's four compass points have a basic symbolical significance. The inhabitants of Nordkalotten are physically dominated by the north and mentally drawn to the south: they are apprehensive of the east and sympathetic to the west. Yet for all the varying winds that blow, the attitudes of most appear to chime with the sentiments of Oliver Goldsmith:

The shudd'ring tenant of the frigid zone
Boldly proclaims the happiest spot his own...
Such is the patriot's boast, where'er we roam,
His first best country ever is—at home.

Further Work

There is relatively little publication in English concerning the problems dealt with in this text. The *Atlas of Sweden* (Stockholm, 1953 and in continuation) and the *Atlas of Finland* (Helsinki, 1960) give good impressions of the comparative position of the northern parts of the respective countries. *The Yearbook of Nordic Statistics* (Stockholm, annually) is the most readily available source for comparative statistics. The important series *Nordisk Utredningsserie* (Stockholm) is partly published in English. The following are some of the publications in English used in the preparation of this book:

ASP, Erkki, 'The Finnicization of the Lapps', *Turun Yliopiston Julkaisuja*, B. 100 (1966).
BARTH, Frederick (ed.), *Ethnic Groups and Boundaries* (London, 1969).
—— (ed.), *The Role of the Entrepreneur in Social Change in North Norway* (Bergen, 1963).
COLLINDER, Bjorn, *The Lapps* (Princeton, 1949).
HELLE, Reijo, 'An Investigation of Reindeer Husbandry in Finland', *Fennia*, 4 (1966).
—— 'Tourism in Lapland', *Nordia*, 2 (1970).
KROSBY, H. Peter, *Finland, Germany and the Soviet Union, 1940–1; The Petsamo Dispute* (Madison, Wisconsin, 1968).
KOKKO, Yrjö, *The Way of the Four Winds* (London, 1954).
MALMSTRÖM, Vincent H., *Norden: Crossroads of Destiny* (Princeton, 1965).
MANKER, Ernst, *People of Eight Seasons* (Stockholm, 1963).
NOUSIAINEN, J. and HODGSON, J., *The Finnish Political System* (Helsinki, 1971).
PALOMÄKI, Mauri, 'On the Concept and Delimitation of the Present-Day Provinces of Finland, *Acta Geographica*, 20 (1968).
STONE, Kirk H., 'Swedish Fringes of Settlement', *Annals of the Association of American Geographers*, 52 (1962).
—— 'Finnish Fringe of Settlement Zones', *Tijdschrift voor Economische en Sociale Geografie*, 57 (1965).
—— 'Regional abandoning of Rural Settlement in Northern Sweden', *Erdkunde*, 25, p. 1 (1971).
SOMME, Axel (ed.), *A Geography of Norden* (London, various editions).
VARJO, Uno, 'Development of human Ecology in Lapland and Finland after World War II', *Geoforum*, 5 (1971).
VORREN, Ornulf (ed.), *Norway North of 65°* (Oslo, 1960).
—— and MANKER, Ernst, *Lapp Life and Customs* (Oslo, 1962).
WECKMAN, K. J., 'Production Allocation in Finnish Agriculture', *Suomen maataloustieteellinen seuran julkaisuja*, 117 (1970).

Index

Acerbi, Joseph 13
administration 25–6, 41, 43–4
air transport 8, 43
Alta 12, 13, 14, 15, 22

Bleikvassli 22
Boden 10, 15, 26, 31
Bodö 15
boundaries 30, 41, 45
Brooke, Arthur de Capell 13
Buch, Leopold von 13
building 35

capital 21, 33–5, 37
Celsius, Anders 13
Clark, Edward 13
climate 8, 36
Collinder, Björn 13
conservation 39–40
Crottet, Robert 39
Crowe, J. R. 31

Dass, Peter 47
diet 27
Dunderland 22

ecology 8, 45
education 35, 37, 38, 41, 44
E.E.C. 21, 59
EFTA 59
Elgström, Ossian 39, 46
emigration 17
employment 19, 33, 35

farming 14, 24–6, 28, 37–8
fishing 14, 17, 21–2, 39
forestry 8, 19, 22, 35, 36

Gaimard, Paul 13
Gallén-Kallela Akseli 47
Gällivare 10, 11, 22

Hammerfest 8, 15, 31
Hamsun, Knut 19
Haparanda 15, 31, 39
Harsprånget 24, 25
health 27, 43
Hedin, Sven 31
hydro-electric energy 11, 14, 23–4, 34
hydrography 9–10

ice 35–6

Kalix 19, 24, 35
Karasjokk 38
Karesuando 39
Kautokeino 38
Kemi 15, 24, 35
Kemijärvi 15, 35
Kirkenes 8, 15, 22
Kirovsk 23
Kiruna 11, 15, 23, 41
Kjellén, Rudolf 30, 31
Kokko, Yrjö 47
Kola 7, 11, 13, 17
Kolari 22
Kolosjoki 23
Kåfiord 13, 22

Laestadianism 27, 43
Laestadius, Petrus 19
Laisvall 22
Lapps 10, 11, 12–14, 38
Leino, Eino 47
Lie, Jonas 47
Ligga 24
Liinahamari 30, 39
Linnaeus, Carl 13
Lofoten Islands 17, 36, 38
Luleå 10, 22, 26, 34–5
Lyngen 13

Magnus, Olaus 12
Malmberget 22
Maupertuis, P.L.M. de 13
metallurgy 34–5
military installations 32, 33, 36
minerals 11, 22–3, 32
Mo i Rana 15, 34–5
Monchegorsk 23
Mosjøen 34
Murmansk 11, 23, 31, 32
Myrdal, Gunnar 32

Narvik 15, 22, 31, 34, 41
national parks 39–40
NATO 33
natural gas 32
Neiden 13
neutrality 33–4
Nikkeli 22
Nordic Council 7, 41
Nordreisa 13

oil 32
Oulu (Sw. Uleåborg) 15, 35, 44

Padjelanta 40
Pauluharju, Samuel 39
Petsamo corridor 22, 30
place names 28, 31
planning 35–6
politics 27–8
population, forecasting 17;
    mobility 15–19, 32, 35
Porjus 24

Raajärvi 22
railways 10, 11, 31
Rautarukki 34–5
recreation 39–40
reindeer 14, 37–8
religion 12–13, 27, 43
Rovaniemi 16, 17, 34
Røssåga 34

Salla 9
Sarek 40
settlement 14–16, 26
Skjervöy 37
Skjöldebrand, A. F. 13
Skum, N. N. 47
social services 26
Stora Sjöfallet 40
Sulitjelma 22
Svappavaara 22
Syd-Varanger 34

technology 7, 11, 23, 29, 44
topography 13
Torni (Sw. Torne) valley 41–3
Tornio (Sw. Torneå) 15
tourism 35, 38–9
transport 10–11, 36, 39
Tromsö 15, 44
Tuloma 24
Turi, Johan 47

Umeå 35, 44

Vadsö 13
Vardö 13

winter 8, 11, 35–6, 39–40
World War II 7, 15, 31–2

Älfsbyn 26